INSIGHT POCKET GUIDE

MADRID

D1322660

Discovery CHANNEL

APA PUBLICATIONS
Part of the Langenscheidt Publishing Group

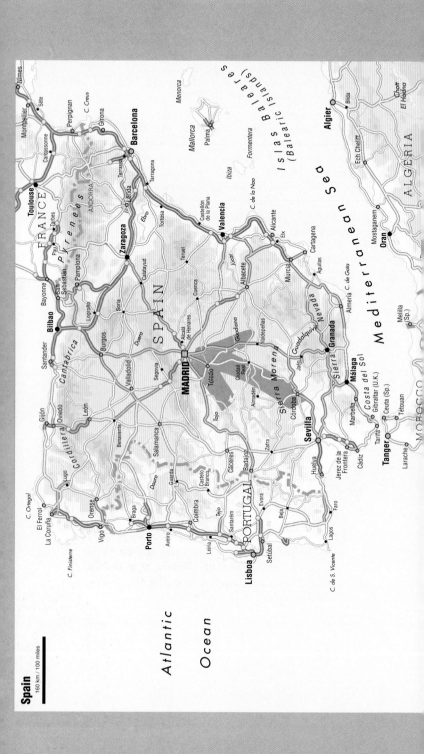

Spain

160 km / 100 miles

Welcome!

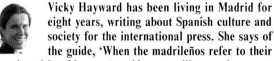

This guidebook combines the interests and enthusiasms of two of the world's best-known information providers: Insight Guides, who have set the standard for visual travel guides since 1970, and Discovery Channel, the world's premier source of non-fiction television programming.

Its aim is to help visitors get the most out of Madrid during a short stay. To this end, Insight Guides' correspondent in Madrid, Vicky Hayward, has devised a range of itineraries to help you make the most of your stay in the city. Three full-day tours take you on a guided tour of the essential highlights – the palaces, the squares, the museums and churches – while the Pick & Mix section offers seven shorter itineraries to suit a range of time-frames and tastes. And, if you want to take a break from the city, three one-day excursions will take you to El Escorial, Segovia, La Granja and Toledo. Complementing the itineraries are an introduction to the city's history and culture, a calendar of special events, chapters on where to find the best shopping, restaurants and nightlife and a fact-packed practical information section.

Vicky Hayward has been living in Madrid for eight years, writing about Spanish culture and society for the international press. She says of the guide, 'When the madrileños refer to their city with pride as *mi pueblo* – my village – they mean it. This is the city I have learned to know through Spanish friends, and I am passing their knowledge on to you in this book.' *Traditional Madrid, royal Madrid, cultural Madrid, religious Madrid, bullfighting Madrid – it's all here. Pick what most appeals.

C O N T E N T S

Pages 2/3:
The Royal
Palace

Pages 8/9: wedding-cake architecture

HISTORY &

Madrid is one of Europe's youngest capitals. 'If you wish to conserve your dominions,' Charles V advised his son Philip II, 'leave the court in Toledo; if you wish to increase them, move it to Lisbon; if you do not mind losing them, take it to Madrid.' Philip ignored his father's advice and in 1561 moved the cumbersome court from the great city of Toledo to the dusty cross-roads town of Madrid.

At the time, Madrid was an agricultural hill-town of some 20,000 people – a third the size of Segovia and a quarter of Toledo – with a reputation for high quality wheat, wine and cheese. Its history reached back only to the 9th century, when a fortress was built here to guard the mountain passes to Toledo. The Muslims gave Madrid its name – 'Mayrít', or 'running waters', referring to its abundant springs and streams – and a maze-like urban layout.

Philip II moved the court to Madrid

For several centuries after Alfonso VI's conquest of Mayrít in 1083, the city remained a hybrid Christian-Muslim satellite of Toledo. It kept its Arab name as well as 'Magerit', the Castilian version, but now the large and wealthy Muslim and Jewish communities lived and exercised their trades outside the walls.

As the fortress town grew into a thriving agricultural and trading community, *arrabales* – new

10

quarters outside the wall – mushroomed. Madrid's rise was marked by the granting of its *fuero*, a town charter laying down citizens' rights and duties (beard-pulling, swearing, and knife-carrying were punishable offences); and by new walls in the 12th and 15th centuries. It was Charles V, cured of a long illness here, who gave Madrid its title *Villa Imperial y Coronada* (Imperial and Crowned Town), and who chose Madrid's Alcázar or fortress as a residence for his son, the crown prince Philip.

Habsburg Madrid

But the town was pitifully ill-equipped to cope with the arrival of the Habsburg court, which brought in its wake the paraphernalia of state and empire, plus courtiers, diplomats, bankers, artists, monks and thieves. Within 40 years the population multiplied five times to reach 100,000. This first deluge shaped much of Madrid's character. Even today most *madrileños* were born elsewhere, making their city a mirror of Spanish regionalism.

Sixteenth-century Madrid mapped out

The Plaza Mayor around 1700

The sudden nature of Madrid's birth also made it a capital of extremes. 'Of Madrid, heaven and earth,' as Cervantes put it. The court's ostentation set a taste for grandeur and conspicuous consumption still evident today. Mule and horse trains loaded down with wine and food for the court rolled in daily, as do today's lorries, from all points around the country. Masquerades, bullfights – then on horseback – royal welcomes, and a string of other fiestas were held in the purpose-built Plaza Mayor. Ever anxious to keep their influence at court, the Church had its own spectacles, such as canonisations (the first was of San Isidro, Madrid's patron saint) and *autos-da-fe* (sacramental plays).

At the same time, handicapped by the lack of a navigable river and by the monarchy's lack of encouragement, Madrid produced almost nothing economically. Chronic unemployment made roguery a way of life and, away from the court and the nobles' houses, convents and monasteries, the majority lived in endemic poverty, lacking the most basic foodstuffs. Despite a new wall built in 1625, overcrowding was so bad that many lived in basements described by an Italian traveller as 'the architecture of moles'. What most caught visitors' attention was the sewage chucked out of the windows after 10 o'clock at night, with a cry of '*¡agua va!*' to give passers-by time to get out of the way. There was no street lighting except on the occasional religious shrine, and no rubbish collection.

The noble Madrid of the Austrias also remained a makeshift city. It had no cathedral or university, and few medieval monuments, except for two bridges against the river's flash-floods. Philip II's energies and vision were expended on the austere palace-mausoleum of El Escorial, outside Madrid. Even in the next century, after the court was a permanent fixture, the style remained plain, mixing cheap brick with expensive stone from the sierra to frame doors and windows fronted by iron railings. Today these classically proportioned buildings have a rigorous beauty. Only in the mid-17th century did the city have an ornamental outburst, *madrileño* baroque, in which rich decoration was set against schematically plain backgrounds under slate roofs.

The tensions between society's grandiose facade and the crumbling decadence behind it were caught by the writers of Spain's Golden Age: Calderón de la Barca, Lope de Vega, Tirso de Molina, and Quevedo, all educated at the Imperial Jesuits' School but who wrote for a theatre tradition as popular with all classes as today's cinema. Royal patronage also made the city a magnet for outsiders: among them, Miguel de Cervantes, whose masterpiece *Don Quixote* satirised the old courtly values, and Diego de Velázquez, whose portraits of the royal family and court capture the dying imperial age of Spain more powerfully than any words.

Age of Enlightenment

The change of dynasties in 1701, after Charles II died without an heir, ushered in many changes. The Bourbons, who are on the throne today (although toppled and restored three times in the intervening centuries), brought with them a centralised reforming monarchy and French 18th-century magnificence to oust Habsburg spiritual austerity. Among the early Bourbons, Charles III, affectionately nicknamed the 'king-mayor', left a particularly strong mark on Madrid. Streets were paved, cleaned and lit. Begging and gambling were controlled, and the famous *serenos*, or night-watchmen, of Madrid were introduced.

Charles III and his successors were also responsible for giving Madrid its heavily classicist monumentalism: the old post office in the Puerta de Sol, the Astronomic Observatory, Puerta de Alcalá, Hospital de Carlos III (now housing the Reina Sofia art centre), Hospicio de San Fernándo (now the Municipal Museum), the Conde Duque military barracks and the tobacco factory all date from this time, their original functions reflecting the state's new role in the Age of Enlightenment. The single most important architectural bequest was the layout of the Paseo del Prado, a social cat-walk and centre of learning which has steadily accumulated artistic riches that have made it the greatest show-place in Madrid today.

Whilst Madrid was thus becoming a European capital, it was also developing its own *castizo* culture (*see p. 25*), observed by the painter Goya. Anti-Europeanism showed itself in the 1766 revolt against a ban on the cape and sombrero – in reality a move against crime – and came to a head more

Self-portrait by Goya

seriously after the French Revolution, when Ferdinand VII opened the door to Napoleon and ordered the royal family into exile in 1808. This triggered the spontaneous 2nd of May uprising, bloodily put down but fervently adopted since as a symbol of the *madrileños'* spirit of unbowed popular heroism. During the rest of the French occupation Napoleon's brother, nicknamed Pepe Botella – literally Pete the Bottle – tried in vain to woo local Spanish support by laying on fiestas and bullfights and removing taxes on alcohol (hence his nickname), but in vain.

The restoration of the Bourbon monarchy did not bring the hoped-for calm after the storm. Ferdinand VII's court sent many, including Goya, into exile, and Spain swung between absolutism and constitutionalism – a lasting legacy of the French Revolution – throughout the 19th century. It was only the signing of the Constitution in 1876, during Alfonso XII's reign, which marked peace for Madrid.

During that time Madrid remained a largely medieval city to outsiders' eyes, closing its gates at 11pm in summer and even keeping part of its walls until 1871. The ever-cynical writer Richard Ford commented: 'The walls … are of mud, and might be jumped over by a tolerably active Remus; but they were never intended for defence against any invaders, except smuggled cigars.' Washington Irving's impression was also of a capital remote from the rest of Europe. Like other Romantic travellers, he saw local habits, such as the siesta – often taken in the street – food-vendors and farmyard animals, the evening *paseo*, women's *mantillas* and fan-language as the exotica of a southern city.

Seeds of Modernity

In fact the seeds of modernity were sown in this period. Migration from country areas hit by chronic unemployment and periodic famine took the population from 170,000 in 1800 to 500,000 by the end

Goya's 'Execution of the Rioters' commemorates the 1808 uprising

Don Quixote salutes

of the century, and it doubled again by 1930. Alongside this came the first timid signs of late industrialisation – shoe, textile and tobacco factories – and the arrival of the railway, gas street-lighting and running water. To the east of the extending Paseo de Castellana, the Marquis of Salamanca developed the quarter of the same name while liberal reformers created the garden suburb of Ciudad Jardín to the north of that.

The speed of change quickened in the 20th century. In 1910 Gran Vía, the city's first high-sided commercial avenue, cut a swathe through the old town, and in the following 30 years, the Metro and radio arrived and Barajas airport was built. Nevertheless, Madrid remained a relaxed capital, drawing outsiders into its nightly café *tertulias*, open literary and artistic conversations, in which Buñuel, Dalí and Lorca loomed large in the 1930s.

The *madrileños* also witnessed the century's most important national political events: the loss of the overseas colonies in 1898, the proclamation of the republic and the royal family's exile in 1931, the revolution and general strike of 1934, and the beginning of the civil war in July 1936. For three years, Madrid suffered hunger, Nationalist bombardments and alarms, and families were divided by their ideology: the raised arm on the statue of Don Quixote in the Plaza de España was said by nationalists to be giving the salute and by communists to be ordering them to storm the prison. These divisions were to leave deep and long-lasting scars which have still not altogether disappeared.

During the post-war years of hunger, or *años de hambre*, recovery was slow. At that time, Franco's Madrid embodied the most conservative aspects of his centralist dictatorship. The city became closed to European ideas, and many who were against the regime went into exile. Camilo José Cela wrote of 'whole streets of a sinister gaze, with the appearance of lodging men without conscience'.

But from the early 1950s, society was changing radically under the surface. Franco began building up Madrid's industry into what is now the biggest concentration in Spain, and at the same time the increasing importance of transport networks began to show the benefits of Philip II's decision to have a dead-central capital. The city grew again, but with visually archaic taste: first, neo-Habsburg brick buildings around the bombed western fringes of town; then high-rise concrete and glass blocks in place of old palaces on the Paseo de Castellana; and, on the edges of the city, shanty-towns without running water or plumbing. Towards the end of the dictatorship Madrid also became a major centre of political opposition, focused on the universities and the unions.

Movida and Money

When Spain finally emerged from dictatorship after Franco's lingering death in 1975, the pent-up desire for change spun Madrid into two decades of dizzying transformation. Proof that the young democracy was rooted – and that the constitutional monarch, Juan Carlos I, had a crucial role to play – came in 1981, after the failure of an attempted military coup.

Madrid's remaking of itself as a democratic capital rather than a court city owed much to one man: Enrique Tierno Galván, the first socialist mayor, whose 25-year plan encouraged both the recuperation of popular traditions and youth culture, which exploded in the iconoclastic *movida*. Out of the *movida* came fashion and art magazines, rock groups and urban tribes, a frenetic migratory nightlife, much fake liberalism and sexual hedonism, plus the odd genuine vein of creativity, most notably the internationally renowned films of Pedro Almodóvar.

Underpinning all this, especially from 1984, was rapid economic growth, which in the late 1980s became the fastest in Europe. Accompanied by an influx of foreign investment, it gave Madrid a hard-edged money culture, wealthy new suburbs, its own jet-set and one of the highest costs of living in the world. One side-effect of growth outrunning the infrastructure has been chronic traffic congestion; parking is among the most anarchic in Europe.

A frenetic nightlife

More positively, the boom released large sums for a major urban face-lift, interesting new architecture and investment in cultural assets. Outsiders also notice the parallel blossoming of local pride. As a car sticker puts it: *Ser español un orgullo, ser madrileño un titulo.* 'To be Spanish, a pride; to be *madrileño*, a title.'

But for all the brassy gloss, Madrid remains an insecure capital. The urge to make up for lost time is almost tangible. The city strives to be dynamic; *madrileños* are as keen to score points on the political, business and cultural circuits as in football leagues.

It is ironic, then, that Madrid's appeal to outsiders is not its slick new face, but the traces of an older way of life. The energy of life within the *barrios*; the formal details of dress and *politesse*; the *madrileños'* references to *mi pueblo*, my village – all these come naturally here. It is the cheek-by-jowl coexistence of the traditions of the old and the dynamism of the new which makes Madrid what it is: restless and tireless, visually kinetic, maddening one moment and magical the next. And always a case apart.

Historical Highlights

854 Foundation of 'Mayrít' (Madrid) by Mohammed I.

1083–86 Alfonso VI captures Mayrít from the Arabs.

1085 Alfonso VI conquers Toledo.

1109 Alif Ben Yusuf sacks, but does not take, Madrid.

1202 Alfonso VIII sanctions *Fuero de Madrid*, formalising town laws and rights.

1309 Ferdinand IV holds first Cortes in Madrid.

1369 Trastamara dynasty begins; Henry II enlarges the Alcázar.

1465 Henry IV gives Madrid the title 'very noble and very loyal'.

1474 Isabella I of Castile León and her husband Ferdinand of Aragón (the Catholic Kings) take Madrid and move Crown Treasury there.

1480 Inquisition established in Castile.

1492 Expulsion of Jews.

1516–55 Charles I of Spain, Holy Roman Emperor, rules Spain from itinerant court, opening Habsburg dynasty.

1520 Revolt of Commons.

1561 Philip II moves court from Toledo to Madrid.

1563–84 Building of El Escorial.

1547 Birth of the writer Miguel de Cervantes.

1601–6 Court moves to Valladolid, but returns permanently to Madrid.

1609 Expulsion of *moriscos* (converted Muslims).

1619 Completion of Plaza Mayor.

1621–65 Reign of Philip IV.

1625 Work begins on building Madrid's fourth city wall (it lasts until 1860).

1632 The Palace of Buen Retiro is built.

1599–1660 Diego de Velázquez, painter.

1700–13 Victory of Philip, Duke of Anjou, in War of Spanish Succession opens the Bourbon dynasty.

1737–1764 Building of new royal palace on the site of the Alcázar, after it was burned down.

1746–1828 Francisco Goya, painter.

1759–83 Charles III, the 'mayor-king'; extensive building in Madrid.

1800–1900 Madrid's population grows: 170,000 to 500,000.

1808 Charles IV abdicates and French army enters Madrid; on May 2 Madrid rises against the French but the revolt is brutally quashed.

1808–14 War of Independence (Peninsula War), during which Napoleon's brother, Joseph Bonaparte, rules. The French are defeated.

1814–33 Ferdinand VII; restoration of Bourbon dynasty.

1836 and **1855** Disentailment of religious property.

1851 First train service from Madrid to Aranjuez.

1910 Building work begins on the Gran Vía.

1919 Metropolitano, the underground system, opens.

1931–36 The Second Republic is declared, following the abdication of Alfonso XIII.

1936–39 Spanish Civil War.

1939–75 General Francisco Franco rules; city population grows from 1 to 3 million.

1975 Juan Carlos I succeeds Franco; restoration of Bourbon monarchy.

1978 Crown guarantees constitution granting autonomy to regions.

1979 First democratic municipal elections: Enrique Tierno Galván is elected mayor of Madrid.

1980 Madrid's population peaks at 3.16 million residents.

1981 Attempted military coup fails after congress held at gunpoint.

1986 Spain joins the European Union.

1992 Thyssen-Bornemisza Collection opens in Madrid.

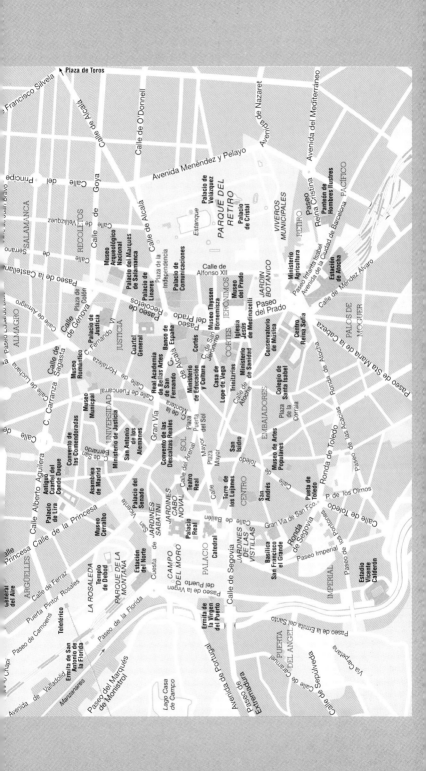

Zero distance

Madrid is a compact capital, but its small, adjacent *barrios*, or neighbourhoods, have very distinct personalities. The itineraries I have assembled in the following pages are designed with this in mind, since it is easy to hop from one *barrio* to another and the contrasts between them – old and new, popular and elegant – are the key to the city's character. The itineraries are also designed to highlight what the city offers best. Three things should not be missed: the visual arts, the nightlife and a glimpse of Castile's old cities.

The itineraries fit around the Spanish day: that is, a long morning until lunch around 2–3pm, after which many – although not all – museums, monuments and workplaces are shut. Eating earlier than 2 or 3pm blocks out several of the few available hours for sightseeing or shopping. For the same reason, the itineraries tend to be busier in the mornings than the afternoons. If you get into Spanish habits – that is lunch as the main meal of the day and long, late nights – you may want the afternoons for siestas.

Moving about in Madrid can be difficult. A car is a positive liability since the city is traffic-choked, and also unnecessary because the Spanish capital is so compact. Walking is often quicker – and more pleasant – than taking buses or taxis. For longer distances the metro is best, as it has a large network covering the entire city. It helps to remember that all street numbering is from the Puerta del Sol outwards. Abbreviations commonly used on maps are **C** (*Calle*), **Av** (*Avenida*), **Trv** (*Travesía*), **P** (*Puerta*), **Pl** (*Plaza*), **P⁰** (*Paseo*) and **Ctra** (*Carretera*).

ARIES

DAY 1

The Heart of Madrid

The old town's squares – including the Puerta del Sol, Plaza Mayor and Plaza de la Villa – and the Convento de las Descalzas Reales; in the afternoon, a tour of late 19th-century Madrid; and in the evening 'tapas' in theatreland.

– Starting point: Metro Sol –

The **Puerta del Sol** is not Madrid's most beautiful square, but it is the city's heart – all distances in Spain are measured from *Kilómetro 0*, marked by a pavement plaque in front of the clock-tower – and the best place to take the city's pulse. It used to be the social centre for thinkers and politicians, but nowadays it exhibits a more marginal and cosmopolitan character. Bullfighting touts, shoppers, pickpockets, buskers and lottery-ticket sellers make a kinetic tableau of Madrid's street life. As Pérez Galdós wrote in the 19th century, here 'anxieties and beliefs meet; society's blood comes and goes, heightening your sensations or draining your strength'.

The square was rebuilt in the mid-19th century around the red-brick post office (1756) – now headquarters of the Comunidad de Madrid – and its name is the only reminder of the city gate decorated with a carved sun (*sol*), which stood here till the 16th century. To-day, its historic profile is hidden by bus-stops, lamp-posts, modern statues and advertising. But the square has other associations. One is the 2

In the Puerta del Sol

The heart of Madrid

320 m / 350 yards

May 1808 uprising, when *madrileños*, poorly armed with guns and knives, and with bricks and furniture to throw out of windows, fought on the streets against the occupying French; the following day, hundreds of Spaniards were shot here in cold blood, a horrific scene immortalised by Goya.

Closer memories are of the Franco years, when many people spent at least a night in the police station, or were badly treated. Today, though, the main association is happier. On New Year's Eve thousands gather here to gobble down a dozen grapes – one for each month – as the ball in the clock-tower drops and midnight chimes.

Taking Calle del Arenal out of the *plaza* (Pastelería Mallorquina, on the corner, makes a good stop-off for coffee and cake), it's a 5-minute walk, via Calle San Martín, second on the right, to the **Monasterio de las Descalzas Reales**, literally Monastery of the Barefooted Royals (Friday and Saturday 10.30am–12.45pm and 4–5.45pm; Sunday 10.30am–12.45pm).

A small corner of the past preserved within high walls, and many *madrileños'* favourite monument, the convent was founded in 1564 by Charles V's daughter, Joanna of Austria, in the palace where she was born. The painted staircase, frescoes, shrines and works of art given in lieu of the blue-blooded nuns' dowries capture the richness of Spain's Golden Age. It is still a working convent, and the kitchen garden is said to produce the most expensive vegetables in Spain, such is the value of the land.

Going back down Calle San Martín, then straight over Calle del Arenal,

In the Monasterio de las Descalzas Reales

down Calle Bordadores, crossing over Calle Mayor and up Triunfo, you emerge in the **Plaza Mayor**, the centre of Habsburg Madrid and a mirror of its social life.

The current *plaza* dates from the end of the 18th century after a fire swept through the earlier wooden buildings in 1790, but its roots go back much further, to the Arab *zoco*, or souk, which grew up on the site of a dried-up lake. In the 15th century it became the town's market place, the Plaza del Arrabal (Square Outside the Walls). The first building was the **Casa de Panadería** (1590, now rebuilt), from which the guild of bakers controlled the prices and consump-

tion of cereals; today it hold the city council's archive. In 1619, Philip III – whose statue stands in the centre of the square – ordered the building of the *plaza* for markets and fiestas. It could accommodate up to 50,000 people, who attended the bullfights and Inquisition executions among other spectacles. The height of the building – six storeys – was revolutionary at the time, inspiring a wave of jokes about people living on top of each other.

For all the transformations it has undergone, the Plaza Mayor has kept its popular character. Today, the most striking new features are the Panadería frescoes, finished in 1992, which show Cibeles, goddess of Madrid, looking for her daughter Proserpine in the underworld. Brilliantly coloured, the semi-erotic images are more 1980s than baroque. In the *plaza* you can still find the typical *sambienás* (hat stores) a Christmas fair and a Sunday morning stamp and old coin market.

Strolling out of the arches around the square, you get intriguing glimpses of old Madrid. Off the southeastern corner stands the **Cárcel del Corte** (1629), today the Ministry of Foreign Affairs, one of the key examples of Habsburg court architecture. Off the other eastern corner, shops in Calles Sal and de Postas have arrays of underwear, flamenco costume, cloth for Holy Week brotherhoods, and fluorescent cribs. Finally, the western corner adjacent to Calle Mayor brings you out by the Mercado San Miguel, a wonderful 19th-century iron and glass market with everything from fruit to ironmongery.

Heading on from here down the Calle Mayor, you come to the **Plaza de la Villa** (laid out in 1463), the medieval centre of government. Originally called the Plaza de San Salvador, after a long-gone church where the medieval council met, the

square's eastern side (on the left as you face it) is home to Madrid's oldest building: the **Torre de los Lujanes**, a 15th-century brick *mudéjar* tower with bands of masonry, big wooden beams (heavily restored at the beginning of the century), horseshoe arches and a splendid Gothic door.

Inside the corner door beyond are the splendid tombs of Beatriz 'La Latina' Galdona, Isabel of Castile's brilliant Latin tutor, and her husband; further in is a carved stone staircase built by Moslem artisans for the hospital founded by La Latina, which gave its name to one of the city's quarters. It is believed that King Francis I of France was kept prisoner here by Charles V after the Battle of Pavia in 1525.

The other buildings in the square were rebuilt in the 16th and 17th centuries with what was seen as more appropriate grandeur: on the south side, the **Casa de Cisneros**, with a magnolia in the courtyard, which replaced the old butchers' guild; on the west side, the **Casa de la Villa** (1640–92) replacing the granary-turned-prison. Today these are occupied by departments of the town hall. Free visits on Monday afternoons allow you to view fine tapestries.

From here, a 20-minute walk down through old Madrid leads you to lunch in one of its taverns. Leaving from the back of the square through the narrow Calle del Cordón – filled by baking smells from the nearby convent – you can jink right at the end, then take the first left down Calle del Rollo, a former parish boundary, to Plaza de la Cruz Verde, where the last Inquisition burning took place.

These quiet streets give a glimpse of Madrid's humble, 17th-century, plaster-and-beam

---

Castizo

Castizo, meaning pure-blooded or authentic, is used to describe anything which captures the *madrileño* character. Its use dates back to the 18th century, when, despite enormous poverty, *madrileños* developed a cheeky swaggering style, dressing more elegantly than they could afford and using exaggerated slang incomprehensible to the outsider. The spirit of this historic *castizo* is well caught in the 19th-century *zarzuelas*, or operettas, and the spring and summer *verbenas* – street-fiestas – for which older people don the traditional costume – checked caps and waistcoats for men, and headscarves plus shawls over long spotty dresses for women – to dance the *chotis*.

More fundamentally, the *castizo* character, which has risen above hardship and even tragedy with humour and bravura, gives Madrid's street-life its wit and cut-and-thrust drama. Quick to take offence, *madrileños* are rarely short of a sharp-tongued ironic retort or roguish facial expression. This street-cockiness is popularly known as *chulería*, which film director Luis Buñuel so aptly defined as 'typically Spanish, made up of aggression, virile insolence and self-sufficiency'.

---

architecture – such as the Casa de Juan Vargas (San Isidro's employer), on the left as you enter the Plaza de Cordón. Alongside these interesting relics of past lives are the grander brick and stone buildings of the nobility, and the more ornate 18th- and 19th-century palaces.

Plaza Dos de Mayo

From the Plaza de la Cruz Verde, follow Calle de Segovia and go down Calle San Pedro to **Plaza de San Andrés**, where there stands the church of the same name, Madrid's best preserved Gothic building, and a small museum dedicated to San Isidro, the city's patron saint. Back up Calle San Pedro, take Calle del Nuncio, lined with old palaces and seigneurial houses. You come out at **Plaza Puerta Cerrada**, so called because the city gate there was kept closed against bandits and smugglers of wine from Valdepeñas. No surprise, then, that it's a traditional centre of bars and restaurants. The most traditional for an *aperitivo* with a *tapa* of *jamón* or cheese (though not cheap) is **Casa Paco**, Pta Cerrada 11.

From here, you can smell the woodsmoke puffing out of Cava Baja, once a defensive ditch outside the city wall. The old coaching inns specialising in wood-oven roasts, which grew up here on the edge of town, include **Posada de la Villa** (*see page 68*) or, if you don't feel like a big meal, **Maxi**, Cava Alta 4, an excellent traditional tavern where you can have a single dish.

After lunch, you may well want to succumb to a siesta. Alternatively, revived by a coffee, you may like to look at another quarter of characterful streets. A short ride on the Metro (Latina to Tribunal) will bring you out opposite the **Museo Municipal**, Calle de Fuencarral 78 (Tuesday to Friday, 9.30am–8pm; Saturday

---

A Short Castizo Dictionary

Chotis: Slow mazurka danced to the barrel-organ in a straight-backed, sedate style, in which the couple's feet should apparently effortlessly remain within the space of a brick.

Chulo: Flashy, slick; also a pimp or gigolo. A *chulapona* is the female equivalent.

Chulear: To tease or insult jokingly.

Chulería: Typically *madrileño* all-knowing attitude towards life.

Finolis: Someone trying to be elegant and 'señorito'.

Lechugino: A lightweight fake, a bluff or dandy (literally a lettuce character).

Piropo: or *requiebro*, a flirtatious and flattering comment.

San Isidro: Madrid's patron saint, a farm labourer canonised along with his wife, whose feast-day is celebrated in May.

Verbena: Popular street-fiestas usually on saints' days, with games, food, and plenty of drink.

and Sunday, 10am–2pm), once the city's orphanage. Its wildly ornate baroque doorway depicts San Fernando, the patron saint of orphans. Behind San Fernando, the museum displays take a light look at Madrid's history, from mammal bones found by the river to the 20th-century city, passing a great model of 17th-century Madrid, maps and paintings.

Calle San Vicente Ferrer, almost opposite, will take you into Malasaña – previously Maravillas – a 19th- and early 20th-century *barrio* with flower-filled balconies, small shops and a lot of bars. It has kept some of its hand-tiled facades: the most amusing are Laboratorios 'Juanse' and the Antigua Huevería, at No 28, both on the corner with Calle San Andrés, and La Industrial.

On Calle San Andrés there's an old *neo-mudéjar* ice factory, which you will pass as you slope down towards the **Plaza Dos de Mayo**, once the gardens of a palace and another flashpoint of the 1808 uprising against the French. It was here, in the artillery barracks, that a 17-year-old girl called Manolita Malasaña, after whom the *barrio* was named, helped her father and his fellow troops load guns for the defence of the barracks, until she was shot down by the bullets of the French.

From here, it's a five-minute walk up Calle Daoiz to San Bernardo – once a university area and the home of noble families – where you can buy delicious biscuits made by the nuns at the **Convento de la Visitación** (San Bernardo 72; 9.30am–1.30pm and 4–8pm).

In the evening, head for the **Plaza Santa Ana** (Metro Tirso de Molina), the centre of theatreland. Redolent with bullfighting associations – Hemingway used to hang out in the **Cervecería Alemana** (No 6) – this is one of the classic quarters to go out for *tapas*. The most picturesquely tiled bar in the city, **Los Gabrieles** (Echegaray 7), is good place for a *fino* or dry sherry. Also worth seeing for its decoration is **Viva Madrid** (Calle Manuel Fernández y González 17). A route around half a dozen

Tiles in Los Gabrieles

bars with different specialities is described on *pages 70–1*, or you can do it the Spanish way and try out places that catch your eye in the side streets.

After that, if you have the energy, there are plenty of nightlife options within a stone's throw: jazz at the **Café Central**, classical music at **La Fídula**, or, from around 1–2am, **Torero** for dancing (*see pages 74–7 for addresses*).

DAY 2

Royal Madrid

In the morning, allow 3 to 4 hours to visit the Royal Palace or the Moslem quarter; after lunch, 2 hours to walk with the 'madrileños' in the Retiro Park amongst fortune tellers and street theatre before cocktails and dinner.

Philip IV in bronze

— Starting point: Metro Opera —

By the 17th century, Madrid had two splendid royal residences: to the east, the Retiro Palace, of which only the gardens remain; to the west the Alcázar, today's Royal Palace, which was rebuilt with Bourbon magnificence in the 18th century. Both enjoy wide horizons where you can appreciate Madrid's dramatically lit skies.

You reach the **Palacio Real** (Royal Palace) from Plaza Isabel II, popularly named Ópera as it is dominated by the vast **Teatro Real** (Opera House). Ever since construction began in 1818 and performances started in 1850, the gigantic theatre has been plagued by structural problems caused by the underground river directly beneath it. In 1998, after a spell

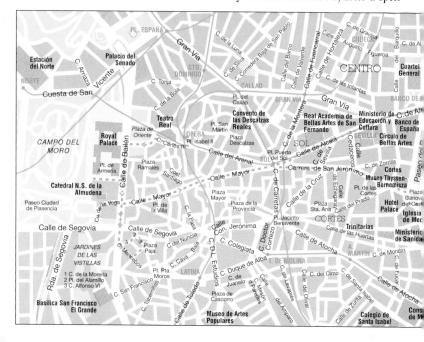

Coffee on the plaza

as a concert hall and lavish refurbishment, it reopened as a state-of-the-art opera house with one of the largest stages in the world. Tickets, which are sold entirely on a season-ticket basis, are like gold-dust; there are guided visits in the mornings.

A good stop-off for breakfast with a view is the **Café de Oriente** (Plaza de Oriente 2), from which you can admire the palace and its square, the largest in madrid. It was laid out on this scale by Napoleon's brother, Joseph Bonaparte, who reigned briefly during the French occupation. Underneath it were the ruins of the medieval royal quarter – including Velázquez's studio – but they were largely destroyed to build a vast underground car park in 1997.

In the centre of the *plaza* stands the 8,150-kg (18,000-lb) equestrian bronze of **Philip IV**, the first statue to solve the difficulties presented by a horse rearing up on its back legs. Designed by Pedro Tacca based on a painting by Velázquez, it was engineered in Italy in 1640, where Galileo solved the problem by recommending that it be made hollow in front and solid at the back. The other statues in the square were made for the top of the palace. There are two theories why they never made it up there: one, that the building couldn't support their weight; the other, backed by local historians, that Isabel de Farnese, Philip V's second wife, refused to allow their elevation after she had a nightmare in which they fell on top of her.

The building of the Palacio Real was begun in 1738 to replace the old Alcázar of the Austrias, which burned down on Christmas Eve 1734. The project was ordered by Philip V, who seized the chance to build a magnificent palace along French-Italian lines. The first king to live there – the building took 30 years to complete – was Charles III and the last was Alfonso XIII, who moved out when he abdicated the throne in 1931. In the interim, the *plaza* was where the monarchy and entourage showed themselves to their people. Here the Italian princess María Antonia de Borbón had her first meeting with her husband Ferdinand VII, about whom she wrote home: 'I thought I would faint. In the portrait he looked rather ugly. Well, compared to the original, the portrait was of an Adonis.'

Today, the palace is still used for entertaining and state events, such as the 1992 Middle East Peace Conference, but most of the time it is open for visits (April to September: Monday to Saturday 9am–6pm, Sunday and holidays 9am–3pm; October to March: Monday to Saturday 9.30am–5pm, Sunday and holidays 9am–2pm; free Wednesday to EU citizens). It has its highlights – the clock collection, some grand 18th-century embroidery, porcelain and glass, Tiepolo's painted ceilings in the Throne Room – but be warned: you walk several kilometres inside, and it's not to every taste. There are also separate small museums in the old Pharmacy, Armoury and Library – and a new Museo Real (scheduled to open in 2002) will display archaeological finds – and wonderful gardens with the carriages museum, reached off the Paseo de la Virgen de Puerto. A good place to stop for a drink en route, though you won't be able to sit down, is **El Anciano Rey de Vinos** (Bailén, 19), which has its own sweet and dry wines.

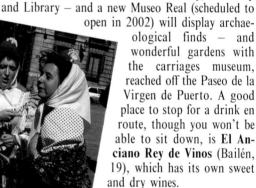

In festival dress

A lighter alternative to the Royal Palace is the little that remains of Arab Madrid. The 19th-century **Catedral de la Almudena**, which was finally finished in 1993, stands on top of the first walled Arab city, and an 11th-century *atalaya* or look-out post has been preserved in the Plaza de Oriente's car park.

If you take the Cuesta de la Vega immediately to the right, you come to the Parque de Emir Mohamed I (down to the left), where you can pick out square towers in a section of the **Arab wall**. The 9th-century sections are of large stones bound with adobe, and the 10th-century ones of masonry, plus later strips of brickwork. Opposite, a plaque marks the site of the Puerta de la Vega, the main entrance to the Arab town, next to which a replica of the Virgin de Almudena is installed where she was (mythically) discovered at the Reconquest. On the other side of the viaduct, Calle de la Morería leads to the **Plaza del Alamillo**, the centre of the Arab quarter after the Reconquest. Its lovely quiet thoroughfares follow hills and curves which have hardly changed since medieval times.

From either here or the palace, head up the **Calle Mayor**, the east-west axis of the Moslem town. As you turn up, you pass on

Recharge in Retiro Park

the right the 17th-century **Palacio de Uceda** (Calle Mayor 79) built by the secretary of Philip III, the Duque de Uceda. Further up, you pass the junction with Calle Traviesa in 1913 where Alfonso XIII and his new wife, Victoria Eugenia, the favourite granddaughter of Queen Victoria, were nearly assassinated when a bomb was thrown down on their wedding carriage. The blood from a decapitated guard splashed through the open window.

A photo of the bombing – and of bullfighters and various other historical incidents – hangs on the walls of **Casa Ciriaco** (Calle Mayor 84), the house from which the bomb was thrown. This is a good place to have lunch, with all sorts of traditional dishes such as chicken *pepitoria* (*see page 69*). If you feel like something more filling, double back to **La Bola** (Calle La Bola 5) for *cocido* (*see page 68*).

After lunch, you can either take the Metro (Sol to Retiro) to the **Parque del Retiro** (Retiro Park) or walk there (30 minutes) along the old royal route: the Calle Mayor and Calle de Alcalá, which takes you past the Real Academia de Bellas Artes de San Fernándo and the Círculo de Bellas Artes (Calle de Alcalá 42), a wonderful place for a coffee in *belle-époque* surroundings. On the diagonally opposite corner of Plaza de la Cibeles is the **Palacio de Linares** (Paseo de Recoletos 2; Tuesday, Thursday and Friday 9.30–11.30am, Saturday, Sunday and holidays 10.30am–12.30pm; fee), a splendid palace (1872–3) built by an ennobled industrialist and now also housing the **Casa de América** cultural centre. The sumptuous neo-baroque interior, the most important of its period in Spain, has recently been restored at a cost of 600 million pesetas, and the ballroom, Chinese room, Byzantine chapel, murals and wooden ceilings are open to the public.

To reach the park from here, continue up to the **Puerta de Alcalá** (1778), built to commemorate Charles

Filling food in La Bola

III's entry to Madrid. In the 1980s it took on a new life, featuring in a rock song as a symbol of the city's new tolerance. Diagonally opposite is one of the main gateways into the **Retiro Park**, which takes its name from '*Buen Retiro*' or Good Retreat, the name given to the bosky Monastery of the Jerónimos after the court took to retiring there at Christmas and Lent. Finally, in 1632, Philip IV built a palace next to it, with huge gardens which opened to the public at the end of the 18th century, and, despite much damage in the War of Independence, became a park in 1868.

The main Avenida Méjico leads up to the boating lake, one of the few surviving elements from the old palace. In royal times, the lake was used for fiestas and extravagant operettas (boating, 10am–sunset). On Sunday mornings and summer afternoons, the paths around the lake are alive with *madrileños* walking their dogs or children, going for a romantic stroll, cruising or having a drink at the kiosks. Among the kiosks, you will find fortune-tellers, joggers, street-theatre, and seasonal attractions; in June, for example, there is a book fair.

Most of the landscaping is now post-18th century: heading right and down from the lake, you come upon the Palacio de Velázquez (1883), built for a mining exhibition, which occasionally holds art

exhibitions from the Centro Reina Sofia; and the romantic Palacio de Cristal (1887), originally a glass-house for exotic plants. Older *madrileños* remember going skating on its lake in winter. Further on, up the Paseo Julio Romero Torres, is the rose garden, stunning from April to June, and, at its western end, the Fal-

The Palacio de Cristal

len Angel (1870s), said to be the world's first statue of the devil. Close by, adjoining the Museo del Prado, is the restored site of the 18th-century Royal Porcelain Factory.

Afterwards have a drink under the splendid modernist stained-glass dome of the **Palace Hotel** (Plaza de las Cortes 7). It was built in 1913, after Alfonso XIII's wedding had shown up the lack of smart accommodation in the city, and the lounge under the dome remains one of the city's most urbane meeting places. It is opposite **Las Cortes**, or the Spanish parliament (1843–50), which has a neo-classical portico guarded by a couple of splendid bronze lions (guided tours Saturday 10.30am–12.30pm). Here, an army colonel held the parliament at gunpoint on 23 February 1981.

The Palace Hotel

From the Palace, it's a 10-minute walk up to dinner at **Lhardy's** (Carrera San Jerónimo 8; tel: 91 5213385; Metro Sol), with its splendid 19th-century dining-rooms and classic cuisine (game, crayfish soup and so on). Started in 1839, this was Madrid's first French restaurant, and cabinet meetings were held here towards the end of the 19th century.

The evening can be continued in the same style at the **Palacio de Gaviria** (Calle del Arenal 9, Metro Sol/Opera; Monday to Saturday 10.30am–3am, to 4.30am Thursday, to 5am Friday and Saturday; Sunday 8pm–2am), a 19th-century palace now converted into a grandly theatrical place to drink and dance.

DAY 3

Metropolis of the Visual Arts

In 1992, Madrid finally realised its grand 18th-century dream of a salon of the arts – a cluster of museums and galleries close together down the city's main avenue. They give a sweeping overview from prehistory to post-modernism which even those who don't consider themselves art-lovers find breathtaking.

– Starting point: Metro Serrano or Retiro. State museums are closed on Sunday afternoon and Monday, except the Centro Reina Sofía which closes on Tuesday. They are free on Saturday afternoon and Sunday, and you can buy a reduced price pass for all three museums –

The small but dazzling **Museo Arqueológico Nacional** (Calle de Serrano 13; tel: 91 5777912; Tuesday to Saturday 9.30am–8.30pm, Sunday and holidays 9.30am–2.30pm; allow 1½ hours for a leisurely visit; fee), is the most undersold of Madrid's museums. Its collection, none

Museo Arqueológico Nacional

of which comes from youthful Madrid, displays the evolution of Iberian culture and extends from a reproduction of the Altamira cave paintings through Iberian stone-carvings (including the famous Dama de Elche, 3rd–4th century BC, an enigmatic sculpture whose gender is a mystery), Roman frescoes and sculptures, the Visigothic crown jewels, post-Reconquest Muslim decorative arts, and Romanesque church sculpture. After seeing these, one looks at Picasso and Miró with different eyes.

From here, cut down Calle Jorge Juan by the Plaza de Colón to the **Paseo de Recoletos**, a section of the city's main north-south avenue. Once a *cañada* – or sheep-track – running alongside a stream on the eastern limits of the city, today it is Madrid's human river, a social boundary: on the Right Bank facing north are the upmarket areas of Salamanca and Retiro; on the Left Bank you'll find the jumbled popular quarters of Centro, Chamberí, Huertas and Atocha. If you feel in need of a cup of coffee, stop off at **Café Gijón** (Paseo de Recoletos 21), Madrid's classic literary café, founded in 1888.

Keeping south, the Plaza de la Cibeles marks the start of the **Paseo del Prado**, laid out in the mid-18th century as an open-air salon where carriages could circulate around a pedestrian promenade and three fountains, all designed by Ventura Rodriguez, fed by the underground stream. At the northern end sits Cibeles (1781–92), Greek goddess of earth, symbol of Madrid; to the south is Neptune (1782), which originally faced Cibeles (Plaza Cánovas del Castillo); and in the centre is Apollo (1777–1803), also known as the Fountain of the Four Seasons, symbolising fire and air (Plaza de la Lealtad). Underlying the classical allegory were other references: at one level, to Charles III's encouragement of agriculture, the navy, arts and sciences; on the other, to the magical symbolism fashionable at court at that

Madrileño matron

time. To this promenade was added first a botanical garden (1781) and then a grand neoclassical museum planned to combine a natural history collection, an academy of sciences, and a congress of scientists. In 1818, Ferdinand VII and his wife Isabel de Braganza decided to house the royal collections of art here, and the collections first opened to the public as the Museo del Prado the following year.

The walk down from Cibeles to the Prado will take you past later grandiose additions built on ex-crown lands: the ornate Palacio de Comunicaciones (nicknamed 'Our Lady of the Posts' for its grandeur); the **Bolsa de Comercio** or stock exchange (1884), with frescoed 19th-century ceilings (Plaza de la Lealtad 1; 11am–noon, free admission) for the ceilings and action on the floor; and, opposite, the Ritz, built after Alfonso XIII's wedding in 1906 revealed the city's lack of aristocratic accommodation. Its wing-collared staff are so strict on security that it's said to be the only place Yasser Arafat is happy to stay without bodyguards.

At the next junction, you come to the **Museo del Prado**, though the main entrance is through the Puerta de Murillo at the far end (Tuesday to Saturday 9am–7pm, Sunday and holidays 9am–2pm; tel: 91 3302800).

The size, range and density of the Prado collection – 8,000 paintings in all – is such that you need repeated visits to digest it in full. In 2001 an ambitious five-storey extension – a stunning design by Rafael Moneo – will further expand the museum's scale, and a reading room will be opened. If you are dipping in for only a few hours, it's a good idea to decide what you want to see. On the one hand, the unique feature of the collection is its breadth, the Spanish monarchs having bought much less locally than the Medicis. Hanging here are some of the greatest works of Bosch, Dürer, Botticelli, Raphael, Titian, Rubens and Rembrandt – and the list could go on. A newly acquired collection 160 Flemish and Dutch paintings (from Van Dyck to Rubens) will hang in the extension. If this is what interests you, buy the *Key to the Prado* by Manuela Mena and Consuelo Luca de Tena as you go in, to locate the works you want to see. Weekly guided tours and private guides are also available.

Velázquez at the Prado

Centro Reina Sofía houses Picasso's 'Guernica'

A second approach, especially rewarding when linked to the other museums, is to concentrate on the native Spanish school. This takes around 2 hours, starting with 15th-century painters such as Juan de Juanes and Pedro Berruguete; moving on to the imported mysticism of El Greco (1541–1614); the religious passion of Ribera (1591–1652) who worked mainly in Naples, and Zurbarán (1598–1664) from Seville; and finally, the work of the two masters whose work is inextricably bound up with Madrid in terms of patronage and what they painted. The first is Velázquez (1599–1660), whose *Las Meninas* is considered by some to be the greatest work of Western art. The second is Goya (1746–1828), whose paintings start with light tapestry designs and end with black horror.

What is so remarkable about looking at these paintings together is what they share: harsh psychological realism, intense light and shade, a looming awareness of death, and – perhaps most striking – the faces and skies you see on the street. Small information sheets on Goya and Velázquez, with basic background facts about their work, are available for a few pesetas as you go round the galleries.

When you need a break, the cafeteria in the basement isn't bad, or you can enjoy the **Jardín Botánico** (Royal Botanical Gardens) (Plaza de Murillo 2; 10am–6pm winter; 10am–9pm summer), or **Atocha Station**'s tropical garden in winter (Plaza Emperador Carlos). For a change of atmosphere at lunch, cross the Paseo and cut up the Plaza Platería Martínez to **El Caldero** on Calle de las Huertas (*see page 69*).

Atocha Station's tropical garden

Another option is to move straight on to the **Centro Reina Sofía** (Calle de Santa Isabel 52; Monday to Saturday 10am–9pm, Sunday 10am–2.30pm; allow 1½ hours), and stop a while in the excellent café there. It is in the Reina Sofia, the new national 20th-century art collection, that the line of inheritance in Spanish painting is really brought home. Nicknamed the Sofidou because of its aim to rival the Pompidou Centre in Paris, it is housed in an 18th-century hospital with flashy hi-tech glass lifts slapped on the front. Here, one huge canvas stands out: Picasso's *Guernica*, painted in a 4-day fury in 1937 after the first deliberate wartime bombing of a civilian population, the Basque town of Guernica, on which incendiary bombs were dropped to burn houses on top of the victims. Picasso would not allow the painting to be brought to Spain until the country was once again a republic. When it finally arrived in 1981 from the Modern Art Museum in New York, it went on show behind bullet-proof glass in an annexe to the Prado, as Picasso expressly wished, then in 1992 it was moved here amid much controversy.

Another highlight of the collection is the gallery devoted to film director Luis Buñuel, the only one of its kind in Europe. Nearly every other 20th-century Spanish artist – notably Dalí, Miró and Antonio López – and a good spread of foreign artists are also represented here, but not always by their best work.

An alternative is the **Museo Thyssen-Bornemisza** (Paseo del Prado 8; tel: 91 3690151, Metro Banco de España; Tuesday to Sunday 10am–7pm; guided tours Tuesday to Friday and Sunday from 3pm), a stunning collection of almost 800 paintings and sculptures from the 13th century to the present day. This museum is widely regarded as the most important private collection in the world. It needs five hours to see the lot, but if you want to dip in, you can pick and choose. The main collection has been laid out chronologically over three floors: at the top are Old Masters; at the bottom is the museum's outstanding 20th-century section, from Soviet Constructivism to Pop Art.

After such a binge of high culture, **Gran Vía** makes a great contrast for the night. Neon, floodlights and huge hand-painted cinema placards – some of the last to survive in Europe – convert it into a garish small Broadway where the *madrileños* love to stroll, buy ice-cream and watch the world roll back and forth. At its eastern end is Chueca, where a great mix of old-fashioned restaurants and modern bars line the narrow streets. You can sip a *mojito* or *daiquiri* to a background of Cuban music in **El Son** (Fernando VI 21, *see page 75*), then it's less than 10 minutes walk to **Casa Salvador** (Calle Barbieri 12), a classic postwar *tasca* (*see page 66*).

The Gran Vía

Option 1. Convents and Churches

You need 3 to 4 hours to see this selection of Madrid's convents and churches. Plainer from the outside than within, they contain everything from medieval 'mudéjar' architecture to stunning baroque frescoes.

– Starting point: Metro Opera –

Until the early 19th century, Madrid was overwhelmingly a monastic and church city. The 18th-century playwright Ramón de la Cruz put these words into the mouth of one of his characters: 'The capital has more churches than homes, more priests than laymen, and more altars than kitchens; even in the entrances of the filthy houses, even in the vile taverns, small paper altarpieces can be seen, along with a medley of wax articles, small basins of holy water and religious lamps.' In part, such religiosity was the inheritance of the Inquisition. Perhaps more important, the religious orders owned an astonishing 75 percent of property in the city until the 19th century, when

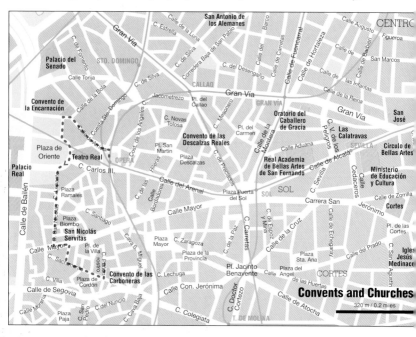

Convents and Churches

320 m / 0.2 miles

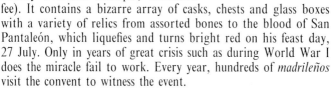

Peddling religion

many of the convents and monasteries were pulled down. Today the *madrileños* are not especially devout, but, even so, religion is a part of everyday life: the outsider's eye picks up on streets named after saints, fiestas marking religious feast days, crucifixes in shops and lobbies, nuns on the street, shops crammed with kitschy religious objects, and formal Easter processions.

The Spanish also love relics. This tour starts at the **Real Monasterio de la Encarnación**, founded by Philip II's daughter-in-law, Queen Margaret of Austria, where there is an extraordinary reliquary room (Plaza de la Encarnación; Metro Opera; Wednesday and Saturday 10.30am–12.30pm, 4–5.30pm; Sunday 10.30am–12.30pm; admission fee). It contains a bizarre array of casks, chests and glass boxes with a variety of relics from assorted bones to the blood of San Pantaleón, which liquefies and turns bright red on his feast day, 27 July. Only in years of great crisis such as during World War I does the miracle fail to work. Every year, hundreds of *madrileños* visit the convent to witness the event.

A short walk across the Plaza de Oriente – where you can have a coffee in the Café de Oriente – and up Calle Lepanto, then down San Nicolás, is the church of **San Nicolás de los Servitas**, the only one of Madrid's original 13 medieval parish churches still intact (Monday 9am–1.30pm, 5.30–8.30pm; Tuesday to Saturday 9–10am, 6.30–8.30pm; Sunday 10am–1.30pm, 6.30–8.30pm; ring the bell in Travesia del Biombo 1 if the door isn't open). It has clear *mudéjar* traces: notably, a fine brick tower – possibly the minaret of an earlier mosque – with a triple layer of blind Moorish arches on ceramic columns; a horseshoe arch; and plasterwork decoration. In one of the side-chapels is an interesting exhibition of medieval Madrid.

Crossing to the other side of Calle Mayor, then right down Calle Traviesa, along Calle del Sacramento and left up the narrow Calle Puñonrostro, is the **Convento de las Carboneras** (Plaza del Conde de Miranda 3, 10am–1pm and 4–7pm), so called because the image of the Virgin was found in a coalyard. The nuns sell delicious small cakes and biscuits, such as *mantecados de jerez* (sherry biscuits). The church itself, which you can also visit, keeps a 17th-century altarpiece by Vincente Carduch. Opposite the convent is a palace

San Nicolás de los Servitas

renowned in the 19th century for selling miraculous Bibles made with the skin of dead children.

If you are interested in architecture, you may like to see a trio of baroque churches built during the building splurge that attended the arrival of the court. Within 10 minutes' walk of each other, they can be visited in succession in the late morning. **San Antonio de los Alemanes** (Corredera Baja de San Pablo 16; Metro Callao; 9am–1pm), built as a hospital for the Portuguese at court

between 1624 and 1633, is covered with 800 sq m (8,600 sq ft) of stunning frescoes by Giordano, Coello and de Ricci. A quarter of an hour's walk away is **Las Calatravas**, built 1686–88, (Calle Alcalá 25; Monday to Saturday 8.30am–2pm and 7.30pm; Sunday 10am–2pm and 7.30pm), with its altarpiece encrusted with garlands, designed and built for the then fabulous sum of 80,000 ducados by José Churriguera. Five minutes down the road from here is San José, built between 1730 and 1742 (Calle Alcalá 43; noon–12.30pm and 1–1.30pm), with an array of polychrome (coloured wood) sculpture, a unique Spanish genre.

This route will also takes you past the finest neoclassical church in Madrid, the **Oratorio de Caballero de Gracia** (Calle Caballero de Gracia 5) which was built 1790–95, (10am–2pm and 5–9pm). Designed by Juan de Villanueva, the 'architect of shadows' and of the Prado, its Corinthian columns are thought to have masonic symbolism. Over the newly restored altar hangs the Cristo de la Agonía,

A bleeding Christ in San José

a baroque masterpiece. Gran Vía was specially re-routed in order to accommodate the church, and the back of the building as seen from Gran Vía shows its bold new post-modernist facade of concrete, marble and glass.

Option 2. The Craft Tradition

A full morning devoted to the city's range of old and new crafts, taking in the Museum of Decorative Arts and a selection of specialist shops.

– Starting point: Metro Banco de España/Retiro –

Even if you do not go in search of Madrid's craft tradition, you will stumble upon it all over the city: *barquilleros* selling wafer cones in the park in summer; *castañeras* with chestnut-roasting barrels in winter; *afiladores* knife-sharpeners, who play whistles to announce their arrival by motorbike; barbers who give double shaves designed to last several days; *zapateros* (shoe menders) repairing rips and tears that seem impossible to mend. All approach their trade as if it were a craft.

And the craftsman's attitude extends to those responsible for dispatching your gifts home. At window No 29 in the central post office, your parcels are carefully wrapped with old-fashioned brown paper, string and hot sealing-wax.

To appreciate the history of the Spanish craft tradition, first spend an hour in the small **Museo de Artes Decorativas** (Calle Montalbán 12; Tuesday to Friday 9.30am–3pm, Saturday and Sunday 10am–2pm; allow 1 hour; fee), where ceramics, wood, textiles and industrial arts, plus a life-size Valencian kitchen, show off their strength as everyday decorative arts. The new **Museo de Artes Populares** (Calle Carlos Arniches 3–5), housed in a restored *corral*, also showcases an interesting array of local crafts, with over 5,000 pieces ranging from costumes to games.

Traditionally, Madrid's craft workshops were clumped in the quarter of old Madrid around the Puerta Cerrada, where muleteers and wagon-drivers came from every region to sell their wares and buy tools and supplies such as bellows, sieves and ropes. It's in this

A guitar-maker's window

quarter too, especially around **Cava Baja** (Metro Latina), that the main vestiges of those traditions survive.

Atanasio Garcia, at Cava Baja 25, sells every conceivable type of string; Salinero, at No 34, ceramics and kitchen hardware; José Goya, a guitar-maker, is at No 42. The woods from which the guitars are made are: palosanto, imported from Brazil and used for the body and hoops; ebony, brought from Gabón and used to make the fingerboard; spruce pine from Germany for the cover; and cedar and cypress from Aranjuez for the handle. Goya also sells picks and strings and organises guitar classes in various styles. Other nearby

Zapatería Tenorio: shoe-maker of distinction

top-quality guitar workshops for those seriously interested in buying are: Paulino Bernabe, at Calle Cuchilleros 8; Manuel González Contreras at Calle Mayor 80; Andrés Martín, at Calle Divino Pastor 22; and Félix Manzanero, at Santa Ana 12, who possesses one of the world's largest collections of guitars, now numbering over a hundred .

Nearby at Calle Toledo 43, the smell of warm wax exudes from **Victor Ortega**, one of the last remaining *cererías*, or candle-makers. Their main trade is still in the long white candles for churches – not expensive – but you can also buy smaller, more decorative ones (the candles are made in the morning only).

At **Zapatería Tenorio** (Plaza de la Provincia 6, tel: 91 3664440), beautiful (but not cheap) handmade country boots and shoes are made; they are accustomed to taking measurements and orders and then sending the finished shoes by post.

All the aforementioned workshops are open from 9.30am–1.30pm and 4–8pm.

Option 3. El Capricho de Alameda de Osuna

A visit to the 18th-century garden at Alameda (minimum 2 hours) and, for those with a car, on to the historic town of Alcalá de Henares where Cervantes was born (about another 2 hours). You may like to take a drink or picnic to the garden; nothing is on sale nearby.

– To the garden: Metro to Canillejas and a 15-minute walk, or by car along NII (beware of traffic jams) and taking exit and signs for Barajas pueblo –

In 1797, the Duchess of Osuna, friend of Goya and arch-rival of the Duchess of Alba, managed to lure Marie-Antoinette's gardener, Jean-Baptiste Mulot, to Madrid, to transform the bare fields on the road to Alcalá de Henares into a Romantic landscape garden. He used the ample water supply from wells to build an artificial river, lake, fountains, and grottoes, creating what Victorian traveller and diarist Lady Holland described in 1803 as 'gardens contrived for coolness'. It later came to be known as El Capricho.

The garden (Saturday, Sunday and holidays: 9am–9pm in summer, 9am–6.30pm in winter) has never looked lovelier. In spring, when the expanse of lilac is a sea of fragrant colour, it's spectacular. Only one warning: many of its best features are fenced off at the time of publication.

Lady Holland also commented on 'innumerable grottoes, temples, chaumières, hermitages, excavations, canals, ports, pleasure boats, islands…' Over the next 50 years, with a brief break during the War of Independence, the Duchess continued the work, hiring Spanish set designer Angél María Tadey to build picturesque architectural features, adding a maze and planting a huge variety of trees. After her death, the garden slowly decayed; the last of the line, Duke Mariano, ruined himself with a series of outlandish extravagances and left so many debts that the garden had to be auctioned in 1896. Finally, it served as an army headquarters in the Civil War and a huge bunker was built underneath. Only in 1974 was the garden salvaged by the town council.

A good approach from the main gates is circular, starting up to the left past the **Old Woman's House**, a beamed cottage with *trompe l'oeil* paintings inside; continuing up to the octagonal **Dance Casino** with its allegorical ceilings, lake and boathouse in the upper English garden; then passing along the artificial river to the model fort, and down through the middle or French garden, to the lilac maze, the **Exedra**, and other various architectural features constructed in the 1790s.

Garden masonry

If you go by car, it's only 20 minutes up the NII motorway to **Alcalá de Henares** (by train or bus, you cannot make the link, but trains go direct from Madrid to Alcalá every 15 minutes, taking half an hour; and buses leave from Avenida de América 34, every 15 minutes and take 40 minutes). A renaissance university town and the birthplace of Miguel de Cervantes, author of *Don Quixote*, it has a fine historic centre despite industrial outskirts. The university buildings

Parque El Capricho

with fine mudéjar decoration (1537–53) are highlights of the Spanish Renaissance; the **Casa-Museo Cervantes** (Calle Mayor; Monday to Friday 10am–2pm and 4–7pm; allow 30 minutes), a reconstruction of Cervantes' childhood home, can be visited; and there are numerous convents, monasteries and churches off the arcaded high street. Of the various old taverns, the **Hostería de Estudiantes** (Calle Colegios 3; tel: 91 888 0330), part of the Parador system, is a beautiful Renaissance building; at weekends it serves thick hot chocolate to put you back on your feet – or, if you go in a large group and book, a Cervantine dinner served by costumed staff.

Option 4. San Antonio de la Florida

Madrid's River Manzanares leads you down to the hermitage nicknamed 'the Sistine Chapel of Spanish impressionism' on account of its Goya frescoes. Allow 4 hours for this, walking back to the city through the Parque del Oeste.

– Starting point: Metro Norte –

The shady riverside terrace starts just below the Estación del Norte, a florid 19th-century railway station (Metro Norte, from Opera). To get to it descend the steps off Paseo de la Florida just opposite the station. In the 1970s this stretch was reclaimed and the duck houses were built by Tierno Galván, Madrid's charismatic mayor. A short stroll takes you down to the Puente de Reina Victoria and the Glorieta de la Florida, where there are cafés (the Florida does good *tapas*) and the hermitage of **San Antonio de la Florida**.

Goya's frescoes

In fact, there are two twin hermitages. The one on the left is a replica, built in 1905 so that Goya's frescoes would be better protected. The original (Monday to Friday 9am–2pm; free admission on Wednesday) was built from 1792. Goya, recognised as the greatest painter of his day through his court paintings, was given a free hand to decorate it. He completed the work in only 4 months, transferring the outlines of sketches on paper into the wet plaster with a knife, painting rapidly on to the wet plaster and then dry-painting on top.

Temple of Debod

At the time of painting these frescoes Goya was recovering from an illness which left him deaf and sardonically critical of frivolous aristocratic Madrid. They show the beginning of a freer, impressionistic style filled with witty and incisive social detail.

The frescoes illustrating the miracle of San Antonio of Lisbon raising a man from the dead broke with the convention of depicting heavenly beings and instead portrayed the people of Madrid: cherubims like street-kids and curvy female angels watch over figures that the artist picked straight out of Madrid society. Restoration began on the frescoes in 1989 to repair the damage done by fire and water during the Spanish Civil War. The restoration work is now finished and the colours – ochres, blues and browns – are back to the rich tones of their former glory.

Under the frescoes is Goya's tomb, erected in 1919 when his body was brought back from Bordeaux, where he died. The skeleton inside is headless, since a Spanish doctor, curious to know what the brain of a genius was like, plundered the tomb in Bordeaux.

Next to the hermitage is **Casa Mingo**, Paseo de la Florida 2 (11am–midnight), an excellent Asturian tavern, cheap and cheerful, where you can eat delicious spit-roast chicken and blue goat's cheese, drink cider and sit outside in the summer. It is packed at weekends. From here you can walk up Calle de Fco Jacinto Alcántara, which runs between the hermitages and over the railway lines, into the Parque del Oeste.

Birds in the hand

At the top of the hill is the **Rosaleda**, or rose garden (open June to November), with its fragrant blocks of colour. Further up the stepped path (to the right of the rose garden as you come out of it), you emerge at Paseo de Pintor Rosales, where you can have a drink at the *terrazas*, or wander along to the nearby **Templo de Debod**, an ancient Egyptian temple. One the highest points of Madrid, this is a good place to see sunsets.

To return, the closest Metro is then Ventura Rodriguez. Alternatively you can pick up the **Teleférico**, or cable car, at the Balcón de Rosales, which will take you down to the Casa de Campo park.

Monument to a passion

Allow 2 hours to visit the bullring and its museum, plus the favourite aficionados' bar, then come back to town to see matadors' suits being made.

– Take the Metro to Las Ventas –

'Nothing,' wrote Jan Morris, 'expresses the mescalin quality of this country better than the bullfight, that lurid and often tawdry gladiatorial ritual, which generally repels the northerner in theory, but often makes his blood race in the act.'

Madrid is one of the world capitals of bullfighting and, even if you would never want to sit through a fight, it is fascinating to glimpse its history and ritual through Spanish eyes at the **Museo Taurino**, or Museum of Bullfighting, in the Plaza de Toros (Tuesday to Friday 9.30am–2.30pm, Sunday 10am–1pm; admission free). In addition, the huge **Plaza de Toros** (Calle Alcalá 231), which holds over 23,000 people and is the second largest bullring in the world after Mexico City, is a monument in its own right, nicknamed 'the cathedral of bullfighting'.

Built in 1929 in brick neo-*mudéjar* style, the ring is decorated around the outside with shields of famous bullrings. At the back of the ring, to the right, is the Patio de Caballos – the horses' courtyard – and the Museo Taurino. The museum, labelled in English and Spanish, doesn't go into the origins of bullfighting (thought to lie in Iberian wedding rituals), but it includes plenty of surprises, such as the 16th-century papal bull laying down excommunication for pro-bullfighting monarchs, and a suit which belonged to Juanita Cruz, the greatest woman bullfighter. There are also paintings and engravings showing the early bullfights in the Plaza Mayor and the 18th-century bullring next to the Puerta de Alcalá, plus the obligatory bulls' heads and heroic portraits of bullfighters.

In the patio opposite the museum is the **Sala de Prensa**, which prints the posters advertising fights. If you go during the season (and sometimes, if you're lucky, out of it) they'll give you one or two recent examples. After your visit, have a drink at **Los Timbales**, Calle de Alcalá 227 (7am–1am), a traditional bar for aficionados that is named after the drums used in the opening ceremony of the bullfight, which are kept here (*see p.age 74* for other taverns).

The only way you can see inside the ring is by going to one of the sporadic rock concerts held here, or a bullfight itself. The season reaches a climax in the 20-day Feria de San Isidro, the world's most important season, starting in the second week of May, when there are also a couple of the horseback *corridas* (*de rejones*). There's a central ticket office at Las Ventas itself (tel: 91 3562200), with prices from 900–11,000 pesetas for the best seats, in the shade, but

Many bars are shrines to the art of bullfighting

they're hard to lay your hands on without recourse to touts. Beware of forgeries. If you do get a ticket, go in *madrileño* spirit with a hip-flask and keep an ear open to the crowd's famously critical banter, then read the write-up on the arts pages of *El País* the following day.

If you don't get a ticket, you can still go to the **Venta del Batán** in the Casa del Campo (Metro Batán), where the the bulls are kept in pens on the day before a fight. From October to May, it is also the venue for the municipal bullfighting school (late afternoon) where young *novilleros* train with capes and straw bulls.

Back in town, you may like to get a closer look at the tailors who make the bullfighters' suits. For £5,000, you can have a suit made. **Sastrería Justo Algaba**, Calle de la Paz 4 (Metro Sol; open 10am–2pm and 5–8pm) and **Angela Gonzalez López**, Plaza General Vera del Rey 11 (Metro Latina), are two of the best.

Option 6. Sunday Morning at the Rastro

A trip to the Rastro flea market can be combined with a look around Lavapiés – the most lively of the old Madrid quarters – and an an 'aperitivo' or lunch in one of the traditional local bars. Allow at least 3 hours.

– Starting point: Latina –

Sunday mornings in Madrid usually mean a long lie-in, a trip to the country or a visit to the **Rastro flea market**, a sprawling hive of stalls and shops with everything from caged birds to snails, books, crafts and clothes.

This extensive and colourful street market runs down from the **Plaza de Cascorro**, named after a battle in Cuba in 1901 at which a Lavapiés orphan, Eloy Gonzalo, heroically

Bargain hunters

Sunday morning at the Rastro

set fire to the walls. A statue in the square depicts him with the rope he attached to himself, so that his fellows could pull back his body if he died.

From here, the market runs down the **Ribera de Curtidores**, and up the side streets, especially the Plaza del General Vara del Rey. Bargaining is the norm on second-hand items (this is often said to be the most African or Arab of the European markets); start a third lower than the price offered and go up from that. Articles for sale tend to be grouped by type. Antiques, for example, are in the Plaza del Rey, Plaza Campillo and the old *rastro* (slaughterhouse), below the Calle del Carnero, after which the market is named. You will also find individual shops in Ribera de Curtidores, such as at Nos 12 and 29.

When you have had enough of the market and the street music – watch out for the gypsy group with a goat and Algerian *rai* (a distinct Arab rock) – you can have a look round **Lavapiés**, named after a fountain for washing feet at the bottom of the quarter. In the 15th century, this was the old *judería* (Jewish quarter), which has left its mark in higgledy-piggledy streets, the remains of a synagogue under the church of San Lorenzo and the saintly Catholic street names given when the Jews were expelled. Still one of Madrid's most characterful working-class quarters, known for its street culture, this has been the birthplace of many bullfighters and much colourful slang.

Take the Calle de San Cayetano (the first left as you go down Ribera de Curtidores), where paintings are sold. At the end, in Calle de Embajadores, is the **Iglesia de San Cayetano** – patron saint of births – its facade by Churriguera and Ribera. On his feast day, 7 August, the saint's image is covered with flowers and paraded

In the atmospheric Lavapiés

around the streets; if you manage to pull off a flower, tradition has it that bread and work are guaranteed for a year. Going on down Embajadores to Calle Sombrerete and the ruins of Santa Catalina, you come to one of the *corralas*, the tall balconied buildings used as popular theatres from the 17th century. This one is currently used for theatre and *zarzuela* as part of the programme of cultural activities organised for Veranos de la Villa.

If your stomach is rumbling by now, there are various options: the **Oso y Madroño** bakery (Calle Caravaca 10) for vegetable and fruit pies; the **Taberna de Antonio Sánchez** (Calle Mesón de Paredes 13), a bar with bullfighting and artistic associations, with good *tapas*; **Nuevo Café Barbieri** (Plaza Lavapiés), one of the oldest cafés in town; or **Los Caracoles** (Plaza del Cascorro 18), for snails and seafood. They're all packed on Sunday lunchtime, but that's part of the attraction. If you feel like going to a restaurant, **Malacatín** (Calle Ruda 5, *see page 68*) is a good choice. It serves great *cocido* and Valdepeñas wines.

Option 7. High-rise Madrid

A bus ride or walk up the Paseo de la Castellana, where high-rise blocks sprout among 19th-century palaces, is something you can do at any time of day. Allow 2 to 3 hours, plus time for a high-rise drink.

– Starting point: Metro Colón –

The **Paseo de la Castellana** has long been a corridor of power. In the 19th century, the tone was set by aristocratic palaces, but today it is dominated by modern banks and office blocks whose value goes up to 600,000 pesetas a square metre.

A good starting point is the massive waterfall of the **Plaza de Colón**. Walk underneath and you are inside a roaring wave which brilliantly evokes Columbus's journey in 1492. Above, skateboarders dodge around a 19th-century statue of Columbus and abstract boat-like sculptures (1977) by Vaquéros Turcos.

Walking north on the same side of the Castellana, you come after six short blocks to the neo-mudéjar ABC building at No

The Torre de Picasso

36–8 and, just above it, an open-air museum of sculpture, curiously tucked under the Eduardo Dato/Juan Bravo flyover. A motley collection, it includes *La Sirena Varada* (1972–3), six tons of cement suspended on iron cords, by celebrated Basque sculptor Eduardo Chillida. Opposite and a little further down, at Nos 29 and

32, are two interesting modern designs: *Bankinter* (1973–76) by Rafael Moneo and a 1979 truncated pyramid.

From here you can take a No 5, 150 or 27 (circular) bus up the Castellana, to the **Plaza de Castilla**. Among the most striking buildings is the Museo de Ciencias Naturales, on your right at

Dramatic Torres Kío

Plaza San Juan de la Cruz. Immediately on your left are the cold grey government buildings of the 1930s Nuevos Ministerios and the 1960s high-rise complex of AZCA. The complex ends at the Palacio de Congresos, with its mosaic frieze by Miró (1980). Opposite is the huge Estadio Santiago Bernabeu, home of football-club Real Atlético.

Another half-dozen stops take you to the Plaza itself, rechristened the **Puerta de Europa** (or Torres Kío) since acquiring two dramatically slanting glass-faced blocks as a northern gateway into the city.

Returning down the other side of the Paseo on the bus – you pay again even if it's the circular No 27 – get off again at AZCA, just after the Congress Hall. One of Madrid's main financial centres, covering 204 hectares (504 acres), it was designed along 1960s American lines. The most interesting of its buildings is the tall BBV (1971–81), No 79–80, built in ochre-coloured aluminium which gradually changes colour as it rusts with age. Designed by Saenz de Oiza, one of Spain's leading modern architects, its foundations are a giant 100-m (330-ft) arch built over the Metro line running underneath. The basement art gallery puts on excellent shows.

The stairs up to the right behind the BBV building take you into paved **gardens** with trees and fountains. From here you see the Alfredo Mau building, a curving wave of glass; the white metallic Torre de Picasso by Minoru Yamasaki, 150m (490ft) high, with 46 floors and five basements; and the Torre Europa, a round tower 31 storeys high, with its own heliport. Unfortunately, none of these or Madrid's other high-rise buildings have public access. For a bird's eye view of Madrid, the best bet is the Faro de Madrid, 92 metres (300 ft) high (Moncloa Metro; June to August: Tuesday to Sunday, 11am–1.45pm and 5.30–8.45pm; September to May: 10.30am–2pm, 5.30–8pm). In summer, you can also head for the Hotel Emperador (Gran Via 53) which has a famous all-day roof terrace with swimming pool and buffet.

EXCURSIONS

Option 8. Excursion to El Escorial

Allow at least 4 hours to visit El Escorial, Philip II's palace. Returning via Franco's Monument to the Fallen takes another 2 hours, or a longer route into the country and past one of the best preserved Roman roads in the world takes another 5 hours.

– To El Escorial: by train (from Atocha, every half hour, journey time 1 hour), or by car along the NVI, taking the El Escorial exit (C505) –

If you travel to El Escorial by car, you can take a detour via **Valdemorillo** (take the El Pardillo turn-off from the C505 onto the C600), a sierra village which has kept its character and some good bars, and arrive at the palace on the road by the Silla de Felipe (*see page 52*). There is easy parking in town, by the palace itself.

The contents of the palace need 2½ hours to see. If you are not going round with a guide, it would be worthwhile reading a guidebook beforehand. If you don't want to go in, you can see the main patios and church without a ticket, and get a feeling of the classical strictness which influences Spanish architecture to the present day.

In 1567, Philip II briefed Juan de Herrera – the chief architect of his planned monastery-palace **El Escorial** – with the following words: 'Above all, do not forget what I have told you – simplicity of form, severity in the whole, nobility without arrogance, majesty without ostentation.'

Whether he achieved this is a moot point. Representing an extreme search for academic truth, stripped clear of all ornament, the palace has always divided opinion. It was received as the eighth wonder of the world, and today some architectural critics see it as an anticipation of modernism. Many others would agree with the

'Majesty without ostentation'

19th-century French writer, Théophile Gautier: 'I cannot help but find El Escorial the most boring and plainest monument of which they, a morose monk and an anxious tyrant, could dream for the mortification of their fellow beings... Few people come back from El Escorial; one dies of consumption there within two or three days, or it burns your brain, even if you're English...'

Undeniably, though, El Escorial (Tuesday to Sunday 10am–7pm, closed Monday; guided groups 10am–12.45pm and 4–7pm, 45 minutes.) is the essence of Spanish history. Its scale is also the most forceful expression of the Spanish urge to absolutism: the giant parallelogram, with twin bell-towers of over 70m (230ft), has 15 cloisters, 16 patios, 88 fountains, 86 stairs, 1,200 doors and 2,600 windows. Also part of the complex are the octagonal marble **Pantheon** of its monarchs (and their mothers), the office from which Philip boasted he ruled the world from two inches of paper, one of the greatest libraries in the West and a superb collection of Old Master paintings.

It adds to a visit if you understand the religious symbolism employed at El Escorial. The site, 56km (35 miles) northwest of Madrid in the foothills of the Sierra Guadarrama, was picked as a meeting point of sky and earth, its northwesterly direction from Madrid symbolic of a meeting with God. Equally, the outer courtyards were built in a grid shape to commemorate Spain's victory in 1557 at St Quentin on the feast day of St Lawrence, who was burnt on a griddle (the legend has it that he turned over when he was done on one side).

The library in El Escorial

After coming out from the palace into the intense light, you can recover in the **Jardín de Frailes** (10am–7pm), the monks' garden beyond the columns on the western side of the palace, and/or go to eat at one of two restaurants: **Charoles**, Calle Floridablanca 24 (tel: 91 8905975), which is excellent but pricey, traditional and *nueva cocina* cooking; or, more cheaply, in **La Cueva**, Calle San Antón 4 (tel: 91 8901516).

El Escorial is now a polite, small town where middle-class families go for the summer. In July it hosts a prestigious summer university and buzzes with life. You can also visit annexes to the main palace, such as the 18th-century **Casita de Arriba**, about 1km (½ mile) from the main palace, and the **Silla de Felipe** (King Philip's Seat). Philip II is said to have used these high rocks as a lookout from which to watch the building works in progress.

The direct route (c600) back to Madrid via the motorway takes you past **Santa Cruz del Valle de los Caídos** (Tuesday to Sunday 10am–6pm, closed Monday), or the memorial built by Franco to

Valley of the Fallen

those who died in the Civil War – the Valley of the Fallen. A chilling parallel to El Escorial, it is another cold exercise in scale – the basilica is carved into the rock under a 150-m (490-ft) cross – with a tank included in the dome mosaic. Many Spaniards resent it as a monument to Franco's dictatorship, and I would not recommend it, but some people admire its engineering.

A marvellous longer alternative by car takes you westwards via Robleda de Chavela (leave El Escorial on the C505 and turn off where marked) and Cebreros, a small wine town, to the **Puerto del Pico** pass (via the N403, C500 and C502). After driving through wonderful valleys of different landscape, you reach the Puerto (after 2 hours), one of the best preserved Roman roads in the world. Below it is the small town of **Mombeltrán** with its medieval castle, a pleasant place to stop for a drink.

Signposted off the same road 5km (3miles) further on are the **Toros de Guisando**, Iberian stone bulls who have lost their horns somewhere along the way. To return to Madrid, continue 30km (19 miles) down the C502 and pick up the NV motorway.

Option 9. Excursion to Segovia and La Granja

You need at least 3 to 4 hours to stroll around Segovia city and visit a few of the sights; after lunch, allow 2 hours for the gardens of La Granja and 3 hours if you include a visit to the tapestry museum. Segovia is always 5–10°C (10–20°F) cooler than Madrid, so you may need to take a warm cover-up.

– It is 2 hours by train to Segovia (irregular departures from Chamartín), 1 hour by bus (Estación del Sur), or 1¼ hours by car, taking the NVI –

Of all the Castilian cities, **Segovia** most easily captures the imagination. Reminiscent of an Italian hill-town, it floats over the plains below like a ship: at its prow rise

The fairy-tale Alcázar

Segovia's cathedral

the angular walls of its turreted castle, at its masthead are the spires of its honey-stoned cathedral and churches, across its stern strides the great Roman aqueduct.

Less darkly historical than El Escorial or Toledo, it makes for a relaxing day out. An accessible small town, it has kept characterful shops, great restaurants – wood-roast lamb and suckling pig are the real reason many *madrileños* come here – and green countryside runs up to the medieval wall. Inside there is much to see: this was a mediaeval court city (Isabel of Castile was proclaimed queen here in 1474) and it has preserved its architectural heritage well.

By car, after passing the Arab watch-tower at Torrelodones, then El Escorial and the Valle de los Caídos off to your left, you pass through the long Guadarrama tunnel built with Republican prisoner-of-war labour. Take the N603 turn-off and, as you run into Segovia, the N110 for Avila. From the aqueduct, the small road marked for La Fuencisla curves around the medieval town wall. Follow the sign to the Alcázar, which is a good place to park.

From here, everything is within easy reach. Both the dramatically sited **Alcázar** (10am–7pm) and the **Catedral** in the centre of town (9am–7pm) are Late Gothic, combining a fairy-tale grace with earlier medieval severities softened by high-pitched turrets and parapets or filigree spires in the case of the cathedral. Both are more rewarding from the outside than the inside, though the cathedral has a serene elegance. Close to the cathedral, at Plaza Mayor No 10, is the tourist office where you can pick up a map.

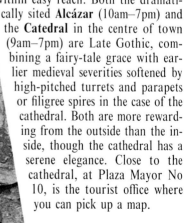

Segovian countryman

54

It is worth trying to get access to a few of the two dozen 12th- and 13th-century Romanesque churches, characterised by Islamic architectural features, tiered bell-towers, arcaded stone galleries where the guilds used to meet, and carved capitals. In the old centre, **San Millán**, **San Martín** and **Santísima Trinidad** are outstanding inside as well as out. Check the changing opening hours at the tourist office. The 18th-century **Palacio Episcopal** (open 10am–2pm) is also worth seeing.

Much of Segovia's attraction is in its small corners and the quirky details you discover as you move around: the arches in Calle Velarde up from the Alcázar; the decorated *seraglio* plasterwork, *mudéjar* brickwork, and tiled street names; the small shops selling embroidery, leather goods and cakes. At the **Convento de las Dominicanas** (Calle Capuchino Alta 2; 9am–1pm, 4–6.30pm), you can buy resin religious figures – mainly angels and saints, such as black Fray Escobar. In Calle Licenciado Peralta 3, there's a wonderful candle workshop, **La Fabril Cerera** (10am–2pm and 5–8pm).

This same street will bring you to the lookouts over the **Acueducto**. Built by the Romans around the turn of the 1st century AD to serve their fortress here, it was originally 14km (8¾ miles) long. The unbound blocks of granite have survived largely because the aqueduct supplied the town's water up until the 1960s. In 1992, the alarm went up that pollution, bird droppings, cars and botched restoration had left the double-arched section close to collapse. After seven years under wraps, the aqueduct has now been unveiled again with a symbolic stream of water carried by it to the city.

Before a late Spanish lunch, you might like to loop the walls. The one-way system leads down and out from the Alcázar on to the Cuesta de los Hoyos (turn right, as for Arévalo), and round under the town's prow to the **Fuencisla sanctuary**, which houses one

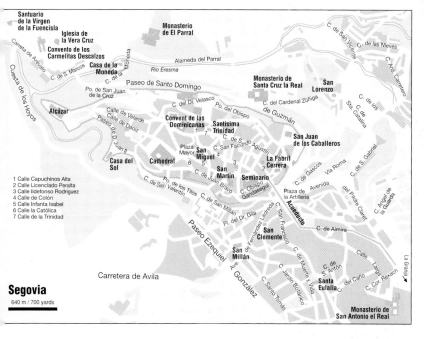

Segovia

640 m / 700 yards

1 Calle Capuchinos Alta
2 Calle Licenciado Peralta
3 Calle Ildefonso Rodriguez
4 Calle de Colón
5 Calle Infanta Isabel
6 Calle la Católica
7 Calle de la Trinidad

of those curious Spanish statues of the Virgin Mary that has a military rank, in this case field-marshal. The Virgin was honoured in 1942 in thanks for saving the town from destruction in the Civil War. Up the next turning (for Zamarramala) is the wonderful **Iglesia de la Vera Cruz** (10.30am–1.30pm, 3.30–6pm), a 12-sided, round-naved Templar church left to shepherds and gypsies for over a century until the Order of St John of Malta took it on in the 1950s. In the inner, top temple is the altar where aspiring knights had to keep a night's vigil watching over their arms. There are good views from the tower.

Continuing round in the same direction, you pass the huge, semi-ruined Santa Cruz church, and fork left down to the village-like quarter of **San Lorenzo**. The Romanesque church sits in a lovely 17th-century *mudéjar* brickwork, plaster and beamed *plaza*, painted ochre and sienna, with the odd shop, café and bar – good for an *aperitivo* and a sense of lócal life.

Wood-roasted lamb, suckling pig and frogs' legs are almost obligatory in Segovia's restaurants. The classic place to eat them is Mesón de Cándido, under the aqueduct (Plaza del Azoguejo 5, tel: 91 428103; 12.30–4.40pm and 8–11.30pm). The historic setting and food justify the prices. Cheaper alternatives abound: for example, the Cueva de San Esteban, behind the Plaza Mayor (Calle Valdeáguila 15; tel: 91 460982; 11.30am–1am; no credit cards).

After lunch take the road (N601) or bus (from the bus-station, Calle Ezequiel Gonzáles, 200m (650ft) from the aqueduct; leaves 1.30pm, 2pm, 3.15pm, and takes 15 minutes) to **Granja de San Ildefonso**. As you leave Segovia, you will pass the monastery of **San Antonio el Real** (open in summer: Monday to Saturday 10am–2pm, 4.30–7pm; Sunday 11am–2pm) on the right-hand side. It has several magnificent *mudéjar* wooden ceilings – and a superb Flemish Calvary.

Strolling in the grounds of La Granja

After some 15 minutes La Granja's elegant slate rooftops appear at the foot of the mountains. Here, Philip V, who had grown up at Versailles, nostalgically built a French-style summer palace (1719–39). More exciting than the ornate interior are the **water gardens** (summer 10am–9pm; winter till sunset) stretching up through sloping woodland behind. The stunning gravity-fed fountains and waterfalls surpass those of many Italian Renaissance gardens. Ornate marble statuary is scattered along paths through elm and chestnut woods graduating to majestic pines encircling a lake. The fountains, some of the highest in Europe, are switched on 3 days a week in late spring and early summer (check with the tourist office for more details, as it depends on the winter's rainfall), but even without the fountains the garden is extraordinarily beautiful. Inside the palace is

the **Museo de Tapices** (Tapestry Museum) (open Tuesday to Friday 10am–1.30pm and 3–5pm; Sunday and holidays 10am–2pm; summer 10am–6pm), which has on display a fine collection of medieval Flemish tapestries.

La Granja is famous for two other things – its 18th-century glass factory, which has been converted into a museum (Fundación Nacional Central de Vidrio; open Wednesday to Sunday, 11am–7pm), and its haricot beans, *judiónes de la Granja*. The beans are buttery-soft because of the soil and water in the region. You can buy them at a grocers or order them for supper at a restaurant, for example at **El Dollar** (Calle Valencia 1; tel: 91 470269; 1.30–4pm and 9.30–11pm).

For a scenic return to Madrid, which is particularly enchanting on a late summer evening, take the

Marble statuary abounds

road through pine forests over the **Puerto de Navacerrada**, the highest pass into Madrid (1,850m/6,000ft).

A second day allows visits to: **Pedraza**, a heavily restored walled medieval village off the N110 north of Segovia, the place to have the best roast lamb; **Sepúlveda**, with Romanesque architecture two centuries older than Segovia's, sitting on a spur between two river valleys; and on to the spectacular **Hoces de Durantón**, a gorge frequented by eagles, with a dam and the small hermitage of San Frutos, all now protected as a natural park. You can then cut across country roads (13km/8 miles) to rejoin the NI at Cerezo de Abajo, 98km (61 miles) from Madrid.

Toledo: former capital of Castile

Option 10. Excursion to Toledo

The city of Toledo is so rich in its history and culture that in a day you can sample only its principal sights; a morning walk around medieval streets and the judería takes about 3 hours; an afternoon visit to the cathedral 1 to 2 hours, depending on your interest.

– By car (N401), it takes only 40 minutes to Toledo. Trains leave every 2–3 hours (1 hour journey from Atocha or Chamartín); buses leave every 30 minutes from 6.30am, from the Estación Sur de Auto-buses, and take 1 hour. It is then 10 minutes by bus from either station into town.

A car is of no use once you're inside Toledo. To avoid crowds, go midweek and, preferably, stay overnight so you can get the feel of the town at night and in the early morning, before the first tourist buses arrive at 9.15am –

Spectacularly sited on a granite rock encircled by the river, **Toledo** is a microcosm of Spanish history: Roman fortress, Visigothic capital and centre of Muslim culture and learning, it reached the zenith of its power after it was reconquered by Alfonso VI in the 11th century and became capital of Castile. For over 3 centuries the Muslims, Jews and Christians lived side by side within its walls, producing a rich, hybrid culture. The court's transfer to Madrid in 1561 began the slow decline which also conserved its astonishing architectural and artistic heritage.

Once inside the city walls, you're in a rabbit-warren of narrow streets, so it's a good idea to buy a city map from a newspaper stand. From the **Plaza de Zocodover**, named after the Arab market, go to the **Mezquita Cristo de la Luz**, the main monument from the early

Marzipan, Toledo's speciality

58

A 'tuna' adds to the medieval flavour

Arab period (kept locked, but you can get the key from Sr. Manzanares, the porter, who also acts as a guide for a small tip). Stepping over the fence, through the quiet garden, you arrive at the heights of the Puerta del Sol, which offers fine views to the north, looking down on two city gates, the Puertas de Bisagra Vieja and Nueva, Muslim and Renaissance respectively.

Close by (opposite the Puertas de Bisagra) is the **Hospital de Tavera** (10.30am–1.30pm and 3.30–6pm), worth visiting if you like palaces and painting. There are works by Titian, Ribera, Zurbarán, Tintoretto and El Greco, as well as a pharmacy, church, library and bedrooms with 16th-century decoration. Make sure you ask to see the complete palace.

Returning to the Puertas de Bisagra, take the Paseo de Recaredo that leads to the 11th-century Puerta del Cambrón, built by Alfonso VI, in which you can see the Arab inspiration under its present Renaissance style. Opposite is the Restaurante del Cardenal inside a 12th-century cardinal's palace, worth peeking into for an *aperitivo*. Close by, No 10 of the Puerta de Cambrón, is a shop selling regional products and offering tastings of Manchego cheese and local wine (prices are reasonable).

From here, the Cuesta de San Martín brings you out at **Monasterio San Juan de los Reyes** (10am–1.45pm, 3.30–5.45pm), one of a series of monasteries founded by Ferdinand and Isabel to com-

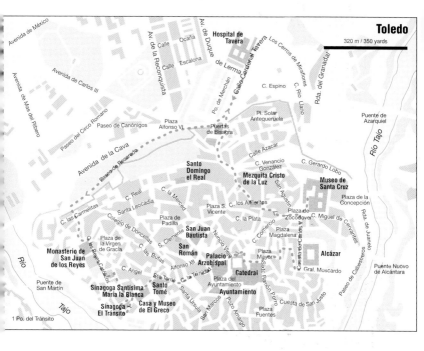

El Tránsito

memorate their military victories. The last major Gothic work in Toledo, it has kept its church, cloister and Arab entrance hall. Following Calle los Reyes Católicos, you enter the *judería*, the old Jewish area of town, where a route is marked by red placards. In the strings of tourist souvenir shops, you may see the world famous Toledan damascene steel being worked.

The prosperity and immunity of the Jewish community came to an abrupt end with the pogroms of 1355. In 1391 there was a massacre at the **Sinagoga Santa María la Blanca** (10am–2pm and 3.30–6pm; summer till 7pm), then the city's main synagogue. It was converted into a Christian church in the 14th century, but has been restored to its original state; the name comes from the white mortar of its walls. At the end of the street, on Calle Samuel Levi, is the second main synagogue, **El Tránsito** (10am–2pm and 4–6pm), founded by Samuel Levi, treasurer to Peter I, in 1366. The finest example of Toledan *mudéjar* architecture, its interior walls are covered by exquisite plasterwork from the Almohad period.

Close by, at Samuel Levi 3, is the **Casa Museo de El Greco** (Tuesday to Sunday 10am–2pm and 4–6pm), the house where the painter is thought to have lived and worked after his arrival in Toledo in 1577. Restored at the beginning of the 20th century and currently under renovation, it possesses 20 of his paintings, but his masterwork, the *Burial of the Conde de Orgáz*, which depicts the apparition of saints Esteban and Agustín against the backdrop of medieval Toledo, is on display in **Santo Tomé church** (10am–5.45pm; summer till 6.45pm), which is close by in Plaza del Conde.

A good place to eat is the **Asador Adolfo**, Calle Granada 6 (tel: 925 227321; open Tuesday to

Corpus Christi in Toledo

Saturday 1–4.30pm and 8pm–midnight), a restaurant in a 14th-century house serving new and traditional Toledan dishes.

In the afternoon, you can turn your attention to the **Catedral** (10.30am–noon and 4–6.30pm), one of the greatest monuments in Spain, with literally thousands of superb artistic and architectural details. To look round it properly takes at least 2 hours – and if you want to understand it fully, it is worth enlisting the services of a guide. The entrance ticket gives you access to the main body of the cathedral. Look out for the splendid carved walnut choir stalls; the frescoed Sala Capitular; the Sacristía Mayor, where there are various works by El Greco; and the Tesoro, a kind of church museum which spells out the church's extraordinary wealth and power. Also worth identifying are the 16th-century stained-glass windows in the rose and side windows of the transept; the magnificent iron screens of the Capilla Mayor; and the opening behind it to let through natural light, known as the *Transparente*.

After so much visual richness, you're unlikely to have the energy for anything except a coffee and a piece of local marzipan. Nonetheless, much remains. If you stay overnight (*see Accommodation, page 86*), another famous sight is the **Alcázar**, the fortress destroyed and rebuilt again and again from Roman times to the Civil War, when it was the scene of great heroism. Madrid's **Museo del Ejercito** is being moved here, as the former building will be an extension of El Prado. Close to the Alcázar, at Calle Cervantes 3, is the **Museo de Santa Cruz** (10am–6.30pm, Sunday till 2pm; closed Monday 2–4pm), a splendid Renaissance building and now the city's fine arts museum, and the **Convento de Santo Domingo El Antiguo** (summer 11am–1pm, 4–7pm; winter open Saturday, Sunday and holidays only), the burial place of El Greco and his wife, where the nuns sell embroidery and jewellery.

> ### Mudéjar Architecture
>
> *Mudéjar*, meaning literally 'surrendered or tributary', is the name given to the architectural style created by Muslim craftsmen who stayed in Spain after the Christian conquest. Muslim building and decorative techniques – Caliphal, Almohad and Nazari – were fused with Romanesque, Gothic and Renaissance features to produce Spain's most original architecture. The earliest *mudéjar* is found in Castile, most notably in Toledo, where the style reached a high-point from the 12th to the 16th centuries. The style was also adopted by the Jewish community after Christian persecution began in the 14th century.
>
> One characteristic of *mudéjar* architecture is the cheapness of its materials – brick, plaster, wood, roofing and ceramic tiles – used to highly decorative effect. Among its most notable features are tiers of pointed or horseshoe arches on minaret-type towers and belfries, and magnificent carved, painted and inlaid wooden ceilings (*artesanados*).

If staying overnight, you might wish to explore the country to the south. A circular route on the N401 leads via **Sonseca** (marzipan), **Orgáz** (14th-century castle) and **Los Yébenes** (traditional leatherwork in the Plaza del Caudillo), past the Toledo mountains (source of the game you find in restaurants), and along the C402 and C403 to **La Puebla de Montalbán**, an historic small town.

Shopping

Shopping in Madrid is especially good for new-wave Spanish design, crafts, second-hand books, guitars and leather goods. The main shopping zones are: **Salamanca**, expensive and elegant; **Gran Vía**, **Puerta del Sol** and **Princesa**, mid-price, with large department stores and Eurochains; and the **old town**, good for crafts.

Opening hours are flexible: 9am–2pm and 5–8pm or 8.30pm; department stores 10am–8pm, though many shops open and close an hour later. Most shops close on Saturday afternoons, but the big department stores stay open and also open on Sundays before public holidays. This can be useful, but is hell!

Flamenco costumes in Calle San Jerónimo

Stores and Malls

El Corte Inglés, with branches at Calle Princesa 42, Calle Goya 76, Calle Preciados 3, Calle Raimundo Fernández Villaverde 79, Calle Felipe II 7 and Calle Alberto Aguilera 39 (tax refunds and shipping facilities, money change, travel agency, RENFE tickets and free maps) is Europe's most profitable department store. You can find almost anything you want there.

Other shopping malls include **La Vaguada** (Metro Barrio del Pilar; 10am–10pm), a vast centre with 350 shops, restaurants and a food market, and **ABC Serrano** (Serrano 61).

Antiques

Madrid's speciality is religious sculptures and objects; much else is imported and overpriced. Shops are grouped around Calle del Prado, and the Rastro, especially on Calle Ribera de Curtidores, which has antiques centres at Nos 12, 15 and 29. In November there is

Calle Ribera de Curtidores

an antiques fair, **Feriarte**, with a growing reputation for properly vetted high quality goods.

Children

Fiestas Paco (Calle de Toledo 52) is a child's dream, with an extraordinary range of party disguises, masks, etc; opposite, at No 55, is **Caramelos Paco**, a huge sweet shop.

Books, Comics, Posters

Madrid is a mecca for book-lovers. The largest bookshop is **La Casa del Libro** (Gran Vía 29), but **Crisol** (main branches at Puerta de la Castellana 154, Goya 18 and Serrano 24; open until 10pm) is more pleasant for browsing. Specialist shops include **Fuentetaja** (San Bernardo 48) for literature and children's books, and **Estanislao Rodriguez** (No 27) for maps, bullfighting books and old prints. For second-hand books, try the stalls on **Cuesta de Claudio Moyano** (also open Sunday), or **Calle Libreros**, just off Gran Vía; for old postcards, posters, etc., head for **Casa Postal** (Calle Libertad 37).

There is an antique book fair in May, and a new book fair 24 May to 11 June in El Retiro.

Crafts

Goatskin wine-bottles: **Julio Rodriguez** (Calle Aguila 12), founded 1907, now run by the third generation. Woodwork: **Florencio Cuadrado** (Ribera de Curtidores 35). Ceramics: **Antigua Casa de Talavera** (Calle Isabel la Catolica 2), founded in the 1920s, for tiles and other Span-

Madrid is excellent for books

ish ceramics. Kitchenware: **Alambique** (Plaza de Encarnación 2). Carpets, rugs and mats: **Alhaba Telar** (Buenavista 33) for original designs in cotton, jute and linen. Haberdashery: **El Botón de Oro** (Juan de Austria 33); braids etc. from the shops in Plaza de Pontejos and Calle Espartero. Shawls and blankets: **Borca** (Mqués Vindo de Pontejos 2). Baskets, mats: **Espartería de Juan Sanchez** (Cuchilleros 9). Hats, uniforms, toy soldiers: **Casa Yustas** (Plaza Mayor 30). Guitars: **Andrés Martín** (Calle Divino Pastor 22) and **Félix Manzanero** (Santa Ana 12) – prices range from 25,000 to half a million pesetas. Cork: **Corchería Castellana** (Calle Colegiata 4).

Antigua Casa de Talaver

At **Artespaña** (Don Ramón de la Cruz 33; Hermosilla 14) craft meets luxury design – beautiful but expensive.

Records

Real Musical (Calle Carlos III 1) for classical; **El Flamenco Vive** (Conde Lemos 7) for flamenco.

Clothes and Fashion

Spanish dress and accessories can be found in small shops around the Puerta del Sol: **Casa de Diego** (Puerta del Sol 12) for fans; **Casa Jiménez** (Calle Preciados 52) for lace shawls, blankets; **Maty** (Calle Hileras 7) for flamenco clothes and dance shoes; **Seseña** (Calle

The ultimate in espadrilles at Alpargatería

de la Cruz 23), founded 1901, for pricey capes and fine embroidered shawls.

Spanish design names are on Calle Serrano (**Adolfo Dominguez**, No 18; **Loewe**, Nos 26 and 34) or close by – **Sybilla** is at Jorge Juan 12 (alley). Calles Almirante Campoamor and the Galería del Prado (Plaza de las Cortes 7) have young designers. The funkiest original clothes are at **Vacas Flacas** (Calle Claudio Coello 24) and **Pepita is Dead** (Calle Dr Fourquet 10). Best budget off-the-peg at **Zara** (Carretas 6 and other branches).

Shoes

For good value, high-quality shoes, go to **Calle Augusto Figueroa**, where shops sell direct from the factory; for high fashion, **Calle Almirante**; for quality, comfort and unusual designs, **Camper** (Gran Vía 54); for all sorts of *alpargatas* (espadrilles), **Casa Vega** (Calle de Toledo 57) and **Alpargatería** (Calle Divino Pastor 29); for high street prices and designs, **Calle Preciados** off Puerta del Sol.

Food and Drink

A good food souvenir is *turrón* – a honey sweetmeat similar to Middle-Eastern *halva*; the very best, bought by weight, come from **Casa Mira** (Carrera de San Jerónimo 30) where *madrileños* queue for hours at Christmas time.

Other edible souvenirs or gifts can be found in supermarkets or El Club de Gourmet departments of **El Corte Inglés** – pricey, but

Sweets in Caramelos Paco

all under one roof – as well as in **Cuenllas** at Ferraz 3 (the best national products). Wine cellars: **Bodegas Santa Cecilia** (Blaxo de Garay 72–4; Metro: Argüelles) for an excellent range at reasonable prices; **Lafuente** (city centre stores at San Bernardo 10, Luchana 28, Quintana 10).

Markets

The many municipal markets are open Monday to Saturday 8am–2pm and 5–8pm. The best are **El Mercado de Chamartín** (Potosí 11; Metro: Colombia), **Mercado de Maravillas** (Bravo Murillo 122; Metro: Cuatro Caminos) and the more select **Centro Comercial La Paz** (Calle Ayala 28; Metro: Serrano). In addition, there is the famous **Rastro street market** on Sunday mornings (*see Option 6*).

Eating

Madrid is a synthesis of the Spanish regions and this is reflected in its restaurants. The city is renowned for receiving the country's best produce by lorry through the night – or even, in the case of fish and seafood, by plane – so all the ingredients are on hand for the full gamut of regional cuisine, including Madrid's own *cocido* (*pot au feu* stew) in traditional taverns or *tascas*, Galician seafood and Mediterranean rices, traditional Basque and Asturian cooking, or, for those who like it, *nueva cocina* (nouvelle cuisine). International cuisine is, by contrast, badly represented and invariably disappointing.

A menu is usually broken down into *primeros platos* or *entrantes* (first courses); these might include *sopas* (soups), *mariscos* (shellfish), *revueltos* (scrambled eggs), *jamón* (chewy air-dried ham), *menestra* (braised vegetables), *pimientos* (peppers) and *queso* (cheese).

Segundos platos, or main courses, usually include *pescados* (fish), *carnes* (meat) and *caza* (game). They usually come without vegetables; if you want some, you need to ask for *verduras* (greens) or an *ensalada* (salad). Look out for *cordero* (lamb) and *perdíz* (partridge) among meats; among the fish on offer look for *merluza* (hake), *rape* (monkfish), *besugo* (bream) and *bacalao* (salt-cod), all of which are common on menus. A *plato combinado* in cafeterias is simply a one-plate meal, invariably served with chips.

Postres (desserts) usually include the ubiquitous *flan*

Flown in from the c

Castilian roasts

(créme caramel), *helados* (ice-creams) and fresh fruit. Coffee comes *solo* (black), *cortado* (a drop of milk) or *con leche* (with a lot of milk).

The *menú del día*, which is usually clipped to the main menu (otherwise ask for it) comes with bread, dessert and wine or water included in the price.

Rioja, Navarra, Valdepeñas, Penedés and Ribera del Duero are the main wine denominations found in restaurants, although smaller ones (eg, Albariño, Rueda and Txacoli for white; Priorato and Ribeiro for red) are interesting to try.

If service and 12 percent IVA (VAT) are not included, this should be clearly stated on the menu.

The concentration of restaurants in the old town – around Plaza Santa Ana, in Centro behind Cibeles, and in the taverns of Cava Baja – includes establishments at every price level, from the 1,000 pesetas lunchtime *menú del día* upwards. The cost of *tapas* can easily mount up to more than you anticipated paying. Fish and seafood are of outstanding quality, but are not cheap. The price categories below are based on a meal for one person with a bottle of wine: £ = less than 4,000ptas; ££ = 4,000–7,700ptas; £££ = more than 7,700ptas.

Unless you like an empty dining-room, you will need to adjust your stomach clock. Opening hours are usually around 1–4pm and 9–midnight, but *madrileños* rarely lunch before 2 or 3pm, or book a dinner table for before 10pm (they fill the intervening gaps by snacking on *tapas*).

You'll often find a business lunch or dinner in progress at a neighbouring table – and not only in smart places if the kitchen turns out good food – but the dress code is casual. A tip of 10 percent is customary.

Nineteenth-century ambience at Lhardy's (see page 71)

Two final warnings: city-centre restaurants close on Sunday and for the month of August; exceptions are listed below. And a surprising number of restaurants don't take any credit cards; where this is the case, this is also mentioned below.

Madrileñan Cooking

CASA SALVADOR
Calle Barbieri 12 (Metro Chueca)
Tel: 91 5214524
Since the 1950s a haunt of bankers and politicians at lunchtime, and artists and night-owls in the evening. Great squid, chicken *pepitoria* (braised chicken in an almond sauce), fish soups, hake and wild boar – among a large choice. £

LA BOLA
Calle La Bola 5
(Metro Domingo/Opera)
Tel: 91 5476930
Famous for its *cocido*, cooked in tall earthenware pots over a wood fire (1,550ptas), and family atmosphere. You will need to book 1–2 days ahead. No credit cards; does not close during summer. £

LA PLAYA
Calle Magallanes 24 (Metro Quevedo)
Tel: 91 4468476
An unpretentious classic for home cooking, with daily specials: *char* (spinach) with potatoes, meatballs, stuffed peppers, homemade puddings. No credit cards. £

MALACATIN
Calle Ruda 5
(Metro La Latina)
Tel: 91 3655241
This restaurant only serves *cocido*, but it is the best you will find in the city. £

POSADA DE LA VILLA
Calle Cava Baja 9
(Metro Tirso de Molina, Latina)
Tel: 91 3661860
One of the most attractive in a street of old inns, serving wood-roast lamb, tripe and other local dishes. Open for Sunday lunch. ££

Other Regional Cooking

AL PIL-PIL
Calle Galileo 21
(Metro Arguelles)

Refreshment at the ready

Tel: 91 4471169
A traditional Basque *tasca* specialising in *bacalao*. £

CASA CIRIACO
Calle Mayor 84
(Metro Sol)
Tel: 91 5595066
One of the most typical *tascas* in the Madrid of the Austrias. Closed Wednesday. ££

DE LA RIVA
Calle Cochabamba 13
(Metro Colombia/Principe de Vergara)
Tel: 91 4588954
Only open weekday lunchtimes, and always packed, but well worth the trip. Superb Castilian home-cooking – beans with partridge, *morcilla* (black sausage) with red peppers, braised vegetables and other dishes – plus house Ribera del Duero. £

EL CALDERO
Calle Huertas 15
(Metro Sol, Antón Martín)
Tel: 91 4295044/0057
Sparkly clean family-owned restaurant that serves Murcian cooking: fish baked in salt and *caldero* (rice and fish) are specialities. Sunday lunch. £

EXTREMADURA
Calle Libertad 13
(Metro Chueca, Banco de España)
Tel: 91 5318958
Great lamb casseroles, wild vegetables, and you can order a trayful of homemade *aguardientes* (eaux-de-vie) from Extremadura. Open Sunday lunch. £

GURE ETXEA
Pl de la Paja 12
(Metro Latina)
Tel: 91 3656149
Among the best traditional Basque cooking in Madrid goes on here, with all the meat, fish and vegetable classics. £££

LA TRAINERA
Lagasca 60
(Metro Serrano)
Tel: 91 5768035/0575
Excellent Galician restaurant featuring fresh fish brought in daily. ££

PARADIS MADRID
Calle Manqués de Cubas 14
(Metro Banco de España)
Tel: 91 4297303
Excellent Catalan cuisine. ££

ST. JAMES
Juan Bravo 26
(Metro Núñez de Balboa)
Tel: 91 5756010
Probably the best rice in the city is served in this Valencian restaurant. ££

Snails a speciality

Traditional tapas bar

Gourmet Cuisine

LA BROCHE
Calle Dr. Fleming 36
(Metro Cuzco)
Tel: 91 4579960
Very upmarket restaurant. The place to go for the best creative cuisine in Madrid. £££

VIRIDIANA
Calle Juan de Mena 14
(Metro Banco de España)
Tel: 91 5234478/5311039
A menu featuring creative Spanish cuisine is complemented by a superb wine list in this rather special restaurant. ££

Other Cuisines

AL-MOUNIA
Calle de Recoletos 5
(Metro Retiro/Banco de España)
Tel: 91 4350828
For something a bit unusual: come here for Moroccan cooking turned into a one-off experience by a wonderful tiled interior. ££

BEEF PLACE
Avenida del Brasil 30
(Metro Cuzco)
Tel: 91 5564187
The first modern Argentinian restaurant to open in the city. Great grilled steaks. £

Vegetarian

Vegetarian dishes are thin on the ground, although *tortilla de patatas* is nearly always available.

The few vegetarian restaurants (all inexpensive) include: **El Vegetariano** (Marqués de Santa Ana 34, tel: 91 5320927; Metro Noviciado/Tribunal) with a changing seasonal menu and salad bar; **Artemisa** (Calle Ventura de la Vega 4, tel: 91 4295092; Metro Sevilla), which is always busy; and **El Granero de Lavapiés** (Calle Argumosa 10, tel: 91 4677611; Metro: Lavapiés), the local favourite.

Tapas Routes

Spanish food is best known abroad for its *tapas* (bar snacks not dissimilar to Greek *mezze*). Strictly speaking such dishes are not all *tapas*, as they come in three sizes: *pinchos* (one mouthful), *tapas* (small snacks) and *raciones* (platefuls). Since the whole point of *tapas* is to *tapear* (hop from one place to the next) I have arranged the following recommendations according to area.

The best times to go to catch everywhere open are noon–2pm and 8–10.30pm.

PLAZA SANTA ANA
A classic *tapas* route, given to me by a Madrid veteran of the *tapas* bar scene, is as follows: **La Toscana** (on the corner of Ventura de la Vega/Manuel Fernández y González 12) for *morcilla de ternera* (veal sausage); **La Chuleta** (Calle Echegaray 20) for griddled mush-rooms or baby lamb chops

Raciones are larger than tapas

La Venencia (Calle Echegaray 7) for marinated olives and salt-dried tuna; **Garrabatu** (Calle Echegaray 5) for Asturian cider, stuffed potatoes or onions; **La Trucha** (Manuel Fernández y González 3) for fried fish, perhaps in *adobo* (marinated), or brains; **Bar Vina P** (Plaza Santa Ana 3) for squid or mussels; **La Casa del Abuelo** (Calle de la Victoria 12) for prawns *al ajillo*; **La Trucha II** (Núñez de Arce 6) for *pimientos* and *champiñones*.

PUERTA DEL SOL

Start at **Casa Bravas** (Pje de Matheu 5), where Madrid's most famous *tapa*, *patatas bravas* (roasted potatoes with peppery sauce), was invented and the recipe for the peppery sauce is still kept a secret; then visit **Lhardy's** (San Jerónimo 8), distinctive for its 19th-century elegance, real consommé from samovars and croquettes from glass cabinets; and finally **Casa Labra** (Calle Tetuán 12), where Pablo Iglesias founded the Socialist Party, also famous for its salt-cod.

CENTRO

El Bocaíto (Libertad 6), which some *madrileños* rate as the best *tapas* bar in Madrid – it's inventive, upmarket and pricey; **Bar Santander** (Calle Augusto Figueroa 25) for *migas* (fried breadcrumbs) as well as canapés and quiches; **Cerveceria Santa Bárbara** (Plaza Santa Bárbara 8) for shellfish and beer; **El Timón** (Calle de Orellana 19) for shellfish.

BILBAO

Calles **Cardenal Cisneros** and **Hartzenbusch** are more studenty and cheaper than the other areas. *Tapas* bars in these streets offer everything from Andalucian fried fish – at **La Giralda** (Hartzenbusch 12 and 15) – to pigs' ears, a Madrid favourite.

For some recommended traditional taverns in different areas, *see page 74*.

La Trucha off Plaza Santa Ana

Nightlife

Madrid is one of the best places in Europe for a night on the razzle. I should warn you that prices are high – 800 pesetas upwards for a drink with music and classy design – and that taxis are hard to pick up on the street by 4am; so call a radiotaxi before leaving a venue.

When in the 1980s Madrid's nightlife was deemed the most exciting in Europe, it was not as newsworthy as outsiders seemed to think. Even the 1202 *fuero*, the first body of local laws, had tried to limit excessive late-night noise, and by the 17th century, the halcyon age of court revelry, every third day was reputed to be a fiesta. In the 19th century, Pérez Galdós, describing Calle Montera off the Puerta del Sol, captured the atmosphere of this: 'the animation was, as always, excessive. It is the mouth of a river of

Reveller in Manolo's, Malasaña

people which chokes against a rising human tide.'

Today, the 1980s' urge to make up for lost time after the repression of the Franco years has lost much of its fizz and the town hall seems determined to kill off what is left. But Madrid's nightlife is still a phenomenon that has to be seen at least once, if only to witness 4am traffic jams and to see the *madrileños* in their element.

The key idea to a *madrileñan* night is to hop around, depending on the time and what you're looking for. A friend from Madrid

The city is electric by night

once joked that you cannot say you have been out for *tapas* unless you have done at least half the number of the stations of the cross – that is, seven bars. It is this restlessness, half spontaneous and half ritualistic, which forms the basis of Madrid's long nights.

The addresses that follow are offered as a core from which to start, but bear in mind that Madrid has over 30,000 bars, and that if you are doing things in the *madrileñan* spirit there is no such thing as a fixed plan. Early evening – that is, 8 or 9pm – is the ideal time to *tapear*, before places are too full, or to visit some of the traditional taverns and *bodegas*. It isn't until after dinner or the cinema, around 11.30pm–midnight, that people begin to move off to the more fashionable music bars (it's hard to get wine in these) and not until 1–2am that they make it to the dance floors.

Around this time of night, when an army of street-cleaners hose down the streets, you remember the old motto '*Madrid me mata*' (Madrid kills me). Bad driving habits, the *madrileños'* boisterous stamina, and conspicuous consumption can all get you down. Drinks, too, get stronger as the night goes on. If you're flagging, a *carajillo* (coffee with a slug of cognac) comes in handy.

In summer, a more relaxing option is a *terraza*, one of the big open-air terrace-bars. These were the hub of nightlife in the late 1980s, turning over up to 5 million pesetas a day from the sale of drinks – everything from *horchata* (tiger-nut milk) and coffee to *cubatas* (gin or whisky and coke), a favourite *madrileño* tipple.

If you make it through to the morning, you can start the next day the traditional way with thick, sweet, hot drinking chocolate and *churros* at **Chocolatería San Ginés**, Pasadizo de San Ginés 5 (open October to May 7pm–7am; June to September 10pm–7am; closed Monday). Otherwise, have an *anis* or cognac to *matar el gusanillo* – kill the worm – as the saying goes, at one of the 24-hour kiosks such as El Arbol, on the corner of Moncloa with the Parque del Oeste.

Traditional Taverns

Madrid has kept a large number of its traditional bars, which are some of the best places to soak up the city's character. This is a brief selection, grouped according to area.

CENTRO
Angel Sierra (Plaza de Chueca 1), a wonderful old tiled bar serving vermouth and beer on tap (the square can feel threatening after dark); **Bodegas la Ardosa** (Calle Colón 13), a range of beers and vermouth on tap from barrels, characterful decor; **Manolo** (Calle Jovellanos s/n, opposite theatre), classic 1930s bar.

SALAMANCA
Peláez (Calle Lagasca 61), one of the few typical bars left in the area. Great canapés and waiters with *hauteur*.

OLD TOWN
Taberna de Antonio Sánchez (Calle Mesón de Paredes 13), classic bullfighting and artists' bar with *tapas* and restaurant; **Taberna El Almendro 13** (Calle del Almendro 13); **El 21** (Calle Toledo 21), picturesquely messy, with beer crates on the bar, liqueurs from all over the world and great deep-fried squid.

Taberna de Antonio Sánchez

Bars and Clubs

Madrid nightlife and culture is more about bars and alcohol than anything else. Below are a few of the perennials in the main areas – **Centro**, **Malasaña**, **Plaza Santa Ana**, and **Moncloa** (students). The best time to go is marked in brackets where it is relevant. Prices can be killing: expect to pay 800–1,000ptas per drink anywhere that has music and decor. At least the recession has brought in happy hours. The *Guía del Ocio*, sold in all kiosks, is the only listings magazine.

Close to the street: **Tupperware** (Corredera Alta de San Pablo 26), comtemporary rock; **La Vía Láetea** (Calle Velaverde 18), a '70s rock 'n' roll institution that never goes out of fashion; **Capote** (Calle Sta. Teresa 3), with a first-class funky DJ; **Torito** (Calle Pelayo 6) for Spanish sounds in an eclectically decorated disco.

For Madrid's bronzed yuppies: **Barnon** (Calle Santa Engracia 17), where Tuesday is Caribbean night and Wednesday funky rhythms, in a luxury venue; **Antigua** (Calle Concha Espina 39), with international DJs; **Teatríz** (Calle Hermosilla 15), with flash Philippe Starck decor; **Le Cock** (Calle de la Reina 16), yuppy/arty crowd.

Hip and relaxed: **Soma** (Calle Leganitos 25), full of corridors and niches; **El Son** (Calle Fernando VI 21), an encyclopaedic selection of rums, fine coffee and friendly company with a background of mostly Cuban music; **Torero** (Calle La Cruz 26; open till 6am), more young-bourgeois and image-conscious; **El 21** (Calle Toledo 21), a popular but unpretentious bar with a selection of over 100 liqueurs; **Star's Café** (Calle Marqués de Valdeiglesias 5), a stylish café-bar with a lively mixed crowd and weekend dancing with DJ.

Quiet havens: **Libertad 8**, at the same address, with piped classical music or live piano when people feel moved to play; **Palacio de Gaviria** (Calle Arenal 9), more expensive but the historic 19th-century backdrop is fantastic.

Terrazas

The summer terraces, sometimes with live music or street theatre, are a unique characteristic of Madrid's nightlife. The action moves on to a new spot every summer, so you need to ask. There are some perennials, however: Plaza Santa Ana is a tourist magnet; Plaza Dos de Mayo is friendly with a chilled-out atmosphere; Lavapiés, in particular, Calle Argumosa, is charming and the *terrazas* are cheaper than elsewhere; in La Latina, terrazas line Plaza de la Cebada; Castellana has a glam atmosphere but is pricey. The terrace bars are usually all closed by 2am.

Club-goers in Malasaña

Dancing

The closest equivalents to the dance scene elsewhere are: **Siroco** (Calle San Dimas 3), with soul and changing DJs, also where all the best local and national bands play; and **Ohm** (Plaza Callao 4), also named **Bash** on Wednesdays, with hip-hop, soul, reggae and funky beats.

Other places are more traditional. Among them are: **El Sol** (Calle Jardines 3), a beloved down-at-heel *movida* haunt with good live nights; **Morocco** (Calle Marqués de Leganés 7), techno disco; **Kathmandú** (Calle S Res. de Luzón 3), a mainstay for acid jazz fans; and **Villa Rosa** (Plaza Sta Ana 15), in a beautiful old flamenco club. In **Kingston's** (Calle Barquillo 29) a diverse, multicultural crowd led by Jamaican hipsters sway to the rhythms of reggae, rap and soul. **Sunstán** (Calle Cruz 7) is one of the most stimulating venues (a bar) in Madrid due to sheer the variety of concerts staged there.

Madrid is strong on salsa. A few addresses are: **Café del Mercado** (Ronda de Toledo 1), which offers one of the most varied selections of Latin music in the capital; **Calentito** (Calle Jacometrezo 15), small and fun though the dancers on the bar bring voyeurs; and **Oba-Oba**, opposite, with tacky decor but real Brazilians (both offer live music).

For insomniacs, there two main after-hours venues: **Goa** (Calle Mesonero Romanos 13), offering high energy techno Friday and Saturday, called **Soul Kitchen** in the early session with funk, rap and soul rhythms; and **Midday** (Calle Amaniel 13), running 9am–3pm on Sunday, and on Wednesday turning into **Nature** from 12am till dawn.

Arts Festivals

Many cultural events take place within the umbrella of arts and theatre festivals, such as: science-fiction cinema (April); classical ballet (December to January); flamenco (April); international theatre (March to April). The **Autumn Festival** combines concerts, theatre, opera and ballet (September to October).

For most events, tickets are available only from the venue itself 5 days ahead. For concerts, tickets are usually sold by **El Corte Inglés** and **Fnac**. Check the newspaper for details.

Live Music

For classical music in Madrid, the **Auditorio Nacional de Musica** (Calle Principe de Vergara 146, tel: 91 3370100) has an excellent programme throughout the year.

For opera, *zarzuela* – a Spanish form of operetta – dance and other musical events, the main venues are the **Teatro Real** (Plaza de Oriente, tel: 91 5160660), the **Teatro de la Zarzuela** (Jovellanos 4, tel: 91 4298225), and **Centro Cultural de la Villa** (Plaza de Colón, tel: 91 5756080). In addition, **Sala La Riviera** (P. Virgén del Puerto) has some good programmes, especially in the August Veranos de la Villa.

Café Central (Plaza del Angel 10) is a jazz landmark, always packed, expensive and a bit pedantic; **Clamores** (Calle Albuquerque

Disco dancing

14) is another venue where some of the best jazz artists play; **La Coquette** (Calle Hileras 14) is the most authentic blues dive in town; and **La Fídula** (Calle Huertas 57) has both piped and live classical music.

Flamenco

In the early spring, during the festival and other theatre seasons, there's good flamenco nearly every night. Tourist *tablaos,* such as **Cafe de Chinitas** (Torija 7) and **Corral de la Morería**, (Morería 17, tel: 91 3658446), are expensive – usually with dinner – and variable. **La Solea** (Calle Cava Baja 27) is a bar with sponteneous performances by locals and tourists.

For truer live flamenco, **Casa Patas** (Calle Cañizares 10) is the place to go. Performers, often from out of town, change every night. On Friday **Peña Chaquetón** (Calle Canarias 39) puts on purist shows.

Flamenco afficionados will want to visit **Viva Flamenco** (Duque de Lemos 7), a shop that sells new and second-hand flamenco CDs, instruments, books, shoes and clothes.

Gay

The Madrid gay scene is always changing. Reliable places to start are: **Why Not** (Calle San Bartolome 6), small but fun, very popular with the locals; and later on **Refugio** (Calle Dr Cortezo 1), for not-to-be missed foam parties, and **Strong** (Calle Trujillo 7, 2am), heavier with a 'dark room'. An alternative is to move about Plaza de Chueca.

Cinema and Theatre

Subtitled movies (labelled v.o.) are plentiful. The main venues are the **Renoir** and **Alphaville** (Calle Martín de los Heros 12 and 14), adjacent **Princesa** (Calle Princesa 3), **Renoir Cuatro Caminos** (Calle Raimundo Fernández Villaverde 10), and **Ideal Multicines** (Calle Dr Cortezo 6). On *el día del espectador* all tickets are cheaper. This is generally Wednesday but find out for individual cinemas through the newspaper or *Guía del Ocio* listings magazine. Theatre is usually in Spanish, except during the autumn festival.

Sex Shows

There are dozens of sex shows (and some of the largest sex shops in Europe). Among these is a women-only male strip at **Charles** (Calle Principe de Vergara 66), and a comic porn show for men in **Erika** (Silva 10). Prostitutes are openly available in Calle La Cruz, Ballesta, Desengano and Montera, and are cheap; Calle Capitán Haya is more upmarket.

Gambling

The **Casino** is a long way out – Carretera de la Coruña *kilómetro* 28,300. Free buses (N6) leave from Plaza España.

Calendar of Special Events

Like every Spanish city, Madrid is enjoying a revival of its fiestas, which include solemn religious processions and over 80 summer *verbenas* (neighbourhood street-parties). Here are a few of them.

JANUARY

Los Reyes Magos: On the night of 5 January, the Three Kings parade through town – arriving by helicopter, camel, etc.

San Antón: At the church in Calle Hortaleza, the blessing of animals takes place on 17 January, the feast day of San Antón.

FEBRUARY

Carnaval: Banned for 50 years by Franco as a threat to public order, Carnival (precedes Lent so depends on the date of Easter) has come back in an uninhibited way, with masked costume (in parades, at parties, on the street), drinking, much transsexual dressing, concerts, etc. The most traditional part is the Ash Wednesday **Burial of the Sardine** (San Antonio de la Florida), a mock funeral an(bonfire.

MARCH

Bullfights: Begin in mid-March an(continue until the autumn.

Easter: Madrid's Semana Santa pro cessions are in the solemn Castilia tradition where religious images ar taken out of the churches and parade(through the streets. The most note worthy processions are outside Madri Chinchón's medieval passion play o Good Friday; Cuenca's dawn Proces sion of the Borrachos (drunks) Toledo's, Avila's and Segovia's atmo spheric silent processions against me dieval backdrops.

MAY

Segundo Mayo: The commemoratio of the 1808 rising against Napoleon i a big local holiday, marked by sport events, concerts, etc.

San Isidro: Madrid's biggest fiesta are for its patron saint. From 8–1 May, the city is alive with *verbena* (open-air dances at night with foo(and drink stalls in different barrios)

...ía de Hispanidad celebrations

bullfight season (the most impor-
nt in the world), a jazz festival,
arathon, open-air theatre, and huge
...ocido cooked in the Plaza Mayor.

Lavapiés and various other quar-
rs, the custom of **May Queens** has
en revived.

JUNE

...an Antonio de la Florida: From
–13 June, single women file into the
...urch to offer a pin in the hope of
...nding a boyfriend; outside, there is
big street party.

...ía del Orgullo (Gay Pride Day): On
...8 June a huge street party spreads
...t from the **Plaza de Chueca**.

AUGUST

San Cayetano (7 August), **San
Lorenzo** (10), **La Paloma** (15): the
most *castizo* of all the *madrileñan* fiestas. In all of them, Virgins are taken
out of the neighbourhood churches
and paraded through the streets, and
the *chotis* is danced to the *organillo*.
Veranos de Villa: During July and
August, open-air concerts, theatre and
dance, including traditional *zarzuela*
and Golden Age theatre in *corrales*
(courtyards).

DECEMBER

Christmas: During December, the
Plaza Mayor turns into a market selling Nativity figures and decorations.
New Year's Eve: One of the biggest
celebrations of the year, when thousands of *madrileños* gather in the
Puerta del Sol for the traditional
eating of 12 grapes while the clock
strikes midnight.

Easter penitents' procession

PRACTICAL information

Atocha Station

GETTING THERE

By Air

Most international airlines have flights to Madrid. The airport (Barajas) is 16km (10 miles) from the centre; buses leave for Plaza Colón every 15 minutes. A taxi will set you back around 2,000ptas; the price may exceed that indicated on the meter, as various supplements are added (*see page 83*). A new Metro line also takes you to the centre, though it may take about 40 minutes. Alternatively, you can rent a car at one of the terminal counters.

By Rail

Two trains leave Paris every night: the Expreso Puerta del Sol, which has turn-of-the-century decor, couchettes, and carries cars; and the Talgo Camas/couchette, more modern and comfortable, with beds. Both

arrive at **Chamartín station**, from whe you can reach the centre by Metro or tax

By Road

The car journey from London and north ern Europe takes a minimum of 24 hour (in a fast car, without an overnight break Allow 6 hours from the Spanish borde at Irún to Madrid. Burgos is a good stop off to visit the magnificent cathedral an eat well. You need a green card, log boo and bail bond, and it's advisable to carr an International Driving Permit.

By Sea

There are ferries from Plymouth to San tander (24 hours) and Portsmouth to Bi bao. The convenience has to be balance against the cost, and in winter the ris of bad weather cancellations. For the Ply mouth to Santander route, contact: Bri tany Ferries, tel: 01752 221321. Fro Santander, you can drive to Madrid vi Reinosa, Palencia and Valladolid, takin in fine Romanesque architecture. Port mouth to Bilbao involves 2 nights on boar Contact: P&O Ferries, tel: 0990 980 98

TRAVEL ESSENTIALS

Passports and Visas

EU Nationals only require a valid na tional identity card. US citizens, Au tralians and New Zealanders require passport and are authorised for a 3-month stay. Visitors from elsewhere require a visa which must be obtained in the Spanish consulate in their own country.

You may prolong your 3-month stay by applying for an extension at the Comisaria de Policia, Sección de Extranjeria, Calle Los Madrazo 9, tel: 91 5219350.

Weather

Madrid's climate is often summed up in the old adage, 'six months of *invierno* (winter) and three months of *infierno* (hell)'. This is an exaggeration: there are two to three weeks of hell (mid-July to the beginning of August), but outside that the dryness makes bearable average daily temperatures of over 30°C/86°F (and up to 45°C/110°F) in summer and 5°C/41°F (down to just below zero) in winter. Rainwear isn't vital – it rains about 50 days a year – but sunglasses are essential. For weather information, tel: 906 365365 (national), 906 365328 (Madrid).

Clothing

Madrileños may be casually elegant, overtly sexy or formally bejewelled, but they are always conformist dressers. Street fashion hardly exists and deliberate scruffiness is not understood or liked. Flesh exposure is okay, short of beachwear in the city.

Electricity

The voltage is 220vAC though a few old buildings still have 120 volts. Two round-pin plugs are standard everywhere, so bring an adaptor if yours are English 3-pin or American flat pin.

Time Differences

Madrid is an hour ahead of Greenwich Mean Time. Noon in Madrid is 11am in

City symbol

London, 6am in New York, 3am in Los Angeles, and 9pm in Sidney. In winter darkness falls around 6pm; in mid-summer around 10pm. For world times, tel: 093.

GETTING ACQUAINTED

Geography

Madrid is the highest capital in Europe (650m/2,130ft), sitting in a dish in the central Iberian plateau, flanked to the north and east by the sierras of Somosierra and Guadarrama, and to the southeast by those of Toledo. The compact city centre is spread over hillocks, with the diminutive River Manzanares running round them to the south. In the last 20 years, huge suburbs dissected by motorways running into the centre have grown around the city.

Government and Economy

Spain is a parliamentary monarchy, ruled by King Juan Carlos I de Borbón since the death in 1975 of dictator General Franco, and governed since 1996 by the conservative Partido Popular (PP). Madrid – the country's administrative, political and economic capital – is currently also in their hands. The city's economy, based on industry since the 1950s, has been fuelled by heavy foreign investment, especially in advanced technologies.

Religion

The majority religion is Catholic, though fewer than 25 percent of Spaniards regularly go to church. Some Catholic churches give foreign language Masses; Madrid also

San José church

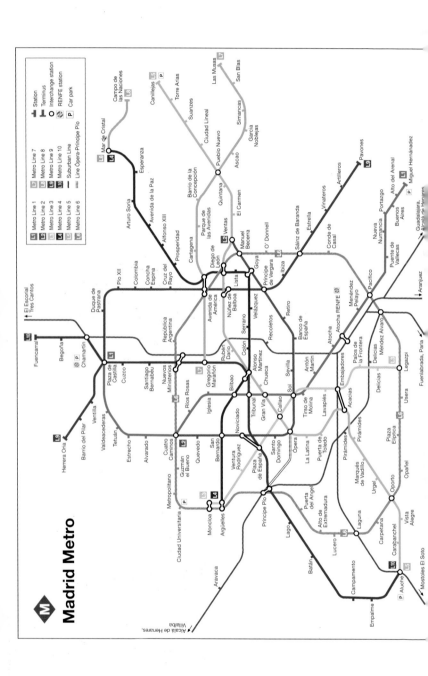

Madrid Metro

has the largest mosque in Europe (M-30), a synagogue (Calle Balmes 3) and there is an Anglican church (St George's, Calle Hermosilla 45) among the 50 non-Catholic churches in the city.

How Not to Offend

Spaniards have an easy-going, familiar kind of courtesy based on common sense rather than etiquette, but they tend to be defensive when they think they are being criticised or laughed at. When speaking Spanish, use the formal *usted*, rather than informal *tú*, for you.

Population

On top of the city's 3 million residents and the province's 5–6 million recorded in the census, there are many more without legal status: gypsies, who live in *chabolas* (shanty-towns); Moroccans, who provide cheap labour and, more recently, other Africans and South Americans.

MONEY MATTERS

Currency

The peseta comes in coins – some irritatingly small – of 1, 5, 25, 100, 200 and 500 pesetas, and notes of 1,000, 2,000, 5,000 and 10,000ptas. People often talk in *duros*, which are worth 5ptas.

Credit cards

A surprising number of restaurants, shops and most petrol stations don't take cards. Visa is the most widely accepted, then Access/Mastercard. You may also have difficulty paying with Eurocheques.

Telebanco cash machines (outside many banks) accept most of the usual cards, but often run out of notes at the end of the month, or at weekends. If you are going out of Madrid for the day, it's best to get cash before you leave. Card cancellations: American Express, tel: 91 5720303; Diner's, tel: 91 5474000; Mastercard, tel: 91 5192100; Visa, tel: 91 5192100. All cards 24-hour cancellation service, tel: 91 5811811.

Tipping

Although service is included in all bills, it is usual to tip in bars and restaurants, and tip guides, taxi-drivers, hotel and station porters, hairdressers and ushers. The size of the tip varies; 5–10 percent in a restaurant, 2–3 percent in a taxi. It is offensive to give a too small a tip.

Changing Money

Most banks are open Monday to Friday 9am–2pm, Saturday 9am–1pm. Note that Cajasde Ahorrs are closed on Saturday, as are all other banks from May to September. Outside these hours, you can change money in Barajas airport, Chamartín and Atocha railway stations, and most four- and five-star hotels. Central Madrid – Gran Vía, Puerta del Sol etc. – also has money-changers (only buying foreign currencies), among which **Check Point**, Plaza Callao 4, is open 24 hours a day.

GETTING AROUND

Street numbers always run outwards from the Puerta del Sol, with even numbers on the right and odd numbers on the left.

Taxis

There are more than 15,000 taxis in Madrid. White with a red diagonal strip, they show a green light on the roof and hang a *Libre* sign in the front window when free. Some operate only as a telephone service (eg **Radioteléfono Taxi**,

Buses run 6am–midnight

tel: 91 5478200/8500 and **Teletaxi**, tel: 91 3712131/3711). The fare shown on the meter is subject to supplements shown on a notice in the back: eg 400ptas to or from the airport; 50ptas for each suitcase; 150ptas between 11pm and 6am and on public holidays and Sundays.

Metro

The quickest way of moving around the city, safe and generally clean, the Metro runs 6am–1.30am. The 10 lines are labelled by number, colour and final destination. Buying a *bonometro*, for 10 journeys on either urban buses or the Metro, saves you up to 50 percent. You can get a Metro map at the ticket booth.

Train

Most suburban trains operate 5.30am–11pm, though some function up to 1am. There are 9 lines to commuter towns, etc., and the main inter-city lines, from three stations: **Chamartín** (for Barcelona, all international trains, Cadíz); **Atocha** (for Seville by AVE – the new high-speed train – Aranjuez, Toledo, Alcalá de Henares and Guadalajara); **Principe Pío/Norte** (for Avila, Galicia, Asturias). These stations are linked by Metro. Phone bookings and information, tel: 91 3289020. The RENFE Central Office, Alcalá 44, is open 9.30am–8pm. Bicycles can be taken on suburban trains only.

Bus

There are more than 150 routes in red and yellow air-conditioned buses, which run from 6am–midnight. Tickets for both are a flat price. The reduced-price ticket for 10 journeys (*bonometro*) can be bought in an *estanco* (tobacconist's/newspaper

A suite at the Ritz

kiosk). Radial night services leave from Cibeles and the Puerta del Sol every half hour midnight–3am and on the hour after 3am Sunday to Thursday, every 2 minutes on Friday and Saturday. Buses for out-of-town trips go mainly from the **Estación Sur de Autobuses** (Calle Canarias 17, tel: 91 4684200; Metro Palos de la Frontera), but check first.

Car

Driving in Madrid is not recommended because of chronic traffic jams, anarchic parking, full car-parks and frequent road works. Never leave a radio or luggage in the car, even in an underground car-park. A car is a blessing for out-of-town trips provided you avoid the four daily rush hours (going in 7.30–9.30am, and at 5pm going out 2–3pm and 8–9.30pm). Beware of on-the-spot speeding fines.

To hire a car, you need to be over 21 and have a current driving licence. Offices are at the airport or in the city centre (**Hertz**, Calle Gran Via 88, tel: 91 5425805; **Europcar**, Calle Orense 29, tel: 91 5559931). A deposit is required unless you pay by credit card.

From September to June, most office hours are 8am–2pm and 5–7pm. Shops are generally open 10am–2pm and 5–8pm. In summer all offices and some shops extend the morning to 3pm and then close in the afternoons. From the end of July, when *madrileños* go on holiday to escape the heat, many smaller businesses are closed.

National holidays are: 1 and 6 January, 19 March, Holy Thursday and Good Friday, 1 May, 15 August, 12 October, 1 November, 6 and 25 December. Local holidays are: 2 and 15 May, 9 November, 7 and 8 December. The city is very quiet Easter week, but less so at Christmas.

The selection below spans Madrid's wide price range, with an emphasis on character. All hotels are required to display prices (including service and tax) at reception and in each bedroom, and to keep a comlaints book (*Hoja Oficial de Reclama-iones*). Staying out of town is much cheaper for the standard of accommoda-ion, and is more peaceful. For help in nding hotels contact the tourist infor-nation desk at the airport or in the Plaza le España.

Prices given below are for double rooms. £ = 6,000–12,000ptas; ££ = 12,000–9,000ptas; £££ = above 19,000ptas.

Madrid

Hotels

AROSA
Calle de la Salud 21, Metro Gran Vía
Tel: 91 5321600
Friendly four-star hotel, just off the Gran Vía. Attracts tour groups. £££

DON DIEGO
Calle Velázquez 45, Metro Velázquez
Tel: 91 4350760
Good value three-star hotel in uptown Salamanca. £

FRANCISCO I
Calle Arenal 15, Metro Sol, Opera
Tel: 91 5480204
Old-fashioned hotel near old Madrid. £

INGLÉS
Calle Echegaray 10, Metro Sevilla
Tel: 91 4296551
Situated near Plaza Santa Ana, theatres and old Madrid. Three-star hotel with garage. £

MONACO
Calle Barbieri 5,
Metro Chueca, Gran Vía
Tel: 91 5224630
Once a classy whorehouse, now an excel-ent two-star hotel, a bargain. Quirky decor. Bar and breakfast café only, but ou are right in restaurant land. £

RITZ
Plaza de la Lealtad, 5
Tel: 91 5212857
Old-style luxury near the Prado. £££

SANVY
Calle Goya 3, Metro Colón
Tel: 91 5760800
Just off Plaza Colón, quiet and comfort-able four-star hotel used by Spanish busi-nessmen, with a pool, fitness centre, and one of the best hotel restaurants. £££

SERRANO HUSA
Calle Marqués de Villamejor 8,
Metro Serrano
Tel: 91 4355200
Small and exclusive in an old-world way, in uptown Salamanca. A four-star hotel, but public rooms are small. ££

TIROL
Calle Marqués de Urquijo 4, Metro Arguelles
Tel: 91 5481900
Good value, three-star hotel famous for its cocktails. Next to Parque del Oeste. £

WELLINGTON
Calle Velázquez 8, Metro Goya, Retiro
Tel: 91 5754400
If you want luxury, this is the most at-mospheric (early 1950s) five-star hotel, tastefully subdued and with strong bullfighting connections. Right by the Re-tiro Park. £££

Hostales

Hostales and *pensiónes* are found all round Madrid for around 1,500–4,000ptas a night, depending on whether you share a bathroom. A good place to start looking is Plaza Santa Ana.

HOSTAL GRECO
Calle Infantas 3, Metro Gran Via
Tel: 91 5224632
Rooms with bathroom and TV.

Youth Hostels

You can obtain youth hostel ID for 500ptas (if under 26) or 1,000ptas, giving access to a network of youth hostels world-wide. Tel: 91 5804242 (10am–2pm) for in-formation, or contact the Youth Hostels Information and Reservation Office: Calle Alcalá 32, tel: 91 5804216.

One of a number of youth hostels or *albergues* in Madrid is:

RECINTO CASA DE CAMPO
Metro Lago
Tel: 91 4635699

You need to be a member; maximum three-night stay. Reduced cost for people under 26 years.

Camping

CAMPING OSUNA
Avenida de Logrono s/n, Metro Canillejas
Tel: 91 7410510
Set in shade-giving pine trees. Bar, restaurant, play-park, food shop and bungalows; rates are low. Open all year round.

Out of Town
Chinchón

PARADOR DE TURISMO DE CHINCHON
Calle Generalísimo 1, tel: 91 8940836
52km (32 miles) from Madrid. A converted 17th-century monastery with beautiful garden and pool in a small historic town. Packed at Easter for the medieval Passion play. *££*

Rascafría

SANTA MARIA DEL PAULAR
Rascafría, tel: 91 8691011
94km (58 miles) from Madrid. Luxury four-star hotel within Castile's first Carthusian monastery, set against the sierra. *££*

Segovia

EL HIDALGO
Calle José Canalejas 3–5
Tel: 921 428190
Restored medieval palace with only seven rooms. Clean and cheap. *Hostal* prices.

LOS LINAJES
Calle Doctor Velasco 9, tel: 921 460475
Well converted, inside an old palace. Good views and close to the Plaza Mayor. *£*

Sigüenza

EL DONCEL
General Mola 1, tel: 949 390001
Simple, clean and within easy walking distance of both the old town and the station. Good restaurant. *Hostal* prices.

PARADOR DE TURISMO DE SIGÜENZA
Plaza del Castillo, tel: 949 390100
Within 17th-century bishop's palace-castle at the top of the town. Great furnishings and garden. *£*

Newsstand at Cibeles fountain
Toledo

EL CARDENAL
Paseo de Recaredo 24, tel: 925 224900
Historic three-star hotel, built by Cardenal Lorenzana in the 18th century. Excellent restaurant. *£*

HEALTH & EMERGENCIES

For general emergencies, tel 112.

General Health

The water in Madrid is good, although there is heavy inner-city pollution. Winter dryness often provokes cold sores and sinus troubles.

Pharmacies

A green or red cross identifies a chemist (*farmacia*). Spanish pharmacists are highly trained paramedics, and are able to deal with many minor ailments. You can freely buy many medicines, including antibiotics, that are available only on prescription in other countries. Outside shop hours go to a *farmacia de guardia*, listed in chemist's windows and in the newspaper. You can also find the nearest *farmacia de guardia* by dialing 098 (general information service).

Medical / Dental Services

If you are an EU citizen and have an E11 form, you will be treated free at *Urgencias* – casualties – in one of the city's large hospitals (La Paz or Ramon y Cajal in the north, Doce de Octubre in the south, or Gregorio Marañón in the centre) or at a local *Ambulatorio,* open 24 hours a day (addresses in the windows of pharmacies and in newspapers). Given long waiting lists and costs, it is a good idea to have private medical insurance. Dental services are not covered by the Spanish national health, and are expensive.

The **Anglo-American Medical Unit** (Calle Conde de Aranda 1, tel: 91 4351823) gives bilingual attention 24 hours a day. For emergency medical care, tel: 061; for poisonings/overdoses, Intoxications, tel: 91 5620420. Emergency hospitals: La Paz, tel: 91 3582831; Ramón y Cajal, tel: 91 3368313; Doce de Octubre, tel: 91 3908000; Gregorio Marañón, tel: 91 5868000.

Crime / Lost Property

You are advised to take the usual precautions to avoid street crime, especially in small side-streets and the Puerta del Sol, a mecca for pickpockets. If you are robbed, report it at the nearest police station (*poner una denuncia*) and fill in a form for insurance purposes. It is always good to have a photocopy of your passport and extra passport-shots with you in case of problems.

Drug-taking in public is strictly forbidden, but hashish (*chocolate/costo*) is sold blatantly on the street in certain areas (notably Plaza de Chueca and Plaza Dos de Mayo, especially at night). Heroin is a major problem, and the main cause of AIDS in Spain.

If you leave something in a taxi, bus, museum or public place, it may be taken to the lost property office (Plaza de Legazpi 7, tel: 91 5884346), but you need to leave a minimum of three days before you can make enquiries.

For police emergencies, phone 091.

Left Luggage

There are offices at the **airport**, **Chamartín** train station, **Estación Sur** and **Plaza Colón** bus stations.

COMMUNICATIONS

Post and Fax

Post offices (*correos*) are open Monday to Friday 9am–2pm and Saturday to 1pm. Alter-

natively, buy stamps in an *estanco* (tobacconist) and use a yellow or red (*express*) postbox. Telegrams are sent from post offices or by phone (tel: 91 5222000). The ornate central **Palacio de Correos**, at Calle Alcalá 50 opposite Cibeles fountain (8.30am– 9.30pm), is much faster than other post offices. For information on all postal services, tel: 902 197197. Most hotels have a fax service, as do photocopy shops and stationers.

Telephone

You can phone from a box (they have instructions in English, but are often out of order), from bars (more expensive, but you don't need the right coins), from hotels (up to four times the normal rate), or from public phone offices (**Palacio de Correos** (*see above*); Gran Vía 30, Puerta de Recoletos 41), where you pay after the call and can use major credit cards. Ring 1003 for Spanish directory enquiries, 025 for international enquiries. To call other countries, first dial the international access code 00 followed by the relevant country code: United Kingdom (44); Canada and the US (1); Australia (61); New Zealand (64); the Netherlands (31); Germany (49), then the area code ignoring any initial 0, followed by the number.

If you are using a US credit phone card, dial the company's access number below, then 01, and then the country code. Sprint, tel: 900 99 0013; AT&T, tel: 900 99 0011; MCI, tel: 900 99 0014.

Media

The most important Madrid papers are: *El País*, serious information, socialist, good foreign coverage; *ABC*, conservative and

Casa de Campo amusements

monarchical, good arts coverage; *El Mundo*, relatively sensationalist but has pioneered serious investigative journalism; *Diario 16*, also sensationalist, more progressive; *La Razón*, conservative, sensationalist. *Guía del Ocio* is a useful, if limited and staid, listings magazine.

Television

There are two state channels, TV1 (mass audience) and La 2 (documentaries, subtitled films, sport). Telemadrid, the regional channel, has city news, football and films.

USEFUL INFORMATION

Children

Madrid is very noisy at night, so make sure you have a quiet hotel room. The Spanish dote on children; they accompany adults to cafés, restaurants and fiestas, even very late at night, and are usually given a warm welcome. See *Attractions* below.

Disabled

Unfortunately, disabled people have no access to buses or the Metro. The five main museums do have disabled access.

Maps

El Aventurero, Calle Toledo 15–17, is an excellent map shop. The Michelin 444 covers a good area around Madrid; FALK plan is the best map of Madrid.

ATTRACTIONS

Descubre Madrid (tel: 91 5882906), part of the Madrid tourist board, offers excellent specialist tours around the city, though mainly in Spanish.

Following is a small selection of museums and other attractions not included in the itineraries:

Aquópolis (Avenida de la Dehesa, Villanueva de la Cañada, tel: 91 8156911). One of the largest Aquatic parks in Europe.

Campo del Moro (Paseo de la Virgen del Puerto; Metro Príncipe Pío). Open daily 10am–8pm, Sundays and holidays 9am–6pm. The gardens of the Royal Palace with two monumental fountains.

Casa-Museo de Lope de Vega (Calle Cervantes 11, tel: 91 4299216; Metro Banco de España/Anton Martín). Open Monday to Friday 9.30am–2pm, Saturday 10am–1.30pm. House of Spain's greatest dramatist from 1610 until his death in 1635.

Centro Cultural de la Villa de Madrid (Plaza de Colón, tel: 91 5756080; Metro Colón/Serrano). Open Tuesday to Friday 10am–9pm, Saturday and Sunday 10am–2pm. Art gallery, two auditoriums, and a café: always something going on.

Círculo de Bellas Artes (Calle Alcalá 42, tel: 91 3605400; Metro Banco de España). Open Tuesday to Friday 5–9pm, Saturday and Sunday 11am–2pm.

Museo de América (Avenida Reyes Católicos 6; Metro Moncloa). Open Tuesday to Saturday 10am–3pm, Sunday and holidays till 2.30pm. Superb collection from the Americas; pre-Columbian to colonial.

Museo de Ciencias Naturales (Calle José Abascal 2, tel: 91 4111328; Metro República Argentina). Open Tuesday to Friday 10am–6pm, Saturday 10am–8pm, Sunday 10am–2.30pm; closed August. Excellent exhibitions on planet earth.

Museo Lazaro Galdiano (Calle Serrano 122, tel: 91 5616084; Metro Nuevos Ministerios). Open Tuesday to Sunday 10am–2pm; July and September also 7.30–11.30pm. Exceptional private collection with enamels, ivories, jewellery and Old Master paintings (Da Vinci, etc.).

Museo Romántico (Calle San Mateo 13, tel: 91 4481071; Metro Alonso Martinez/Tribunal). Open Tuesday to Saturday 9am–3pm, Sunday 10am–2pm; closed Monday, public holidays and August. One of the most interesting small museums.

Museo Sorolla (Puerta General Martínez Campos 37, tel: 91 3101584; Metro Rubén

Darío or Iglesia). Open Tuesday to Saturday 10am–3pm, Sunday 10am–2pm; closed public holidays and August. The beautifully kept house and garden of the Valencian impressionist painter Sorolla.

Parque de Atracciones (Casa de Campo, tel: 91 5268030; Metro Batán). Open Saturday noon–11pm, Sunday and holidays noon–1am. Highest rollercoaster in Europe, live concerts in summer.

Planetario (Pque Tierno Galván, tel: 91 4673898; Metro Méndez Alvaro). Shows Tuesday to Sunday, 11.30am, 12.45pm, 5.30pm, 6.45pm and 8pm (in winter Tuesday to Friday 5.30pm and 6.45pm only).

Real Academia de Bellas Artes de San Fernándo (Calle de Alcalá 13, tel: 91 5221491; Metro Sol/Sevilla). Open Tuesday to Friday 9.30am–7pm, Saturday to Monday 9.30am–2.30pm. Five centuries of Spanish painting, including works by El Greco, Goya, Alonso Cano and Zurbarán.

Teleférico (Paseo de Pintor Rosales, tel: 91 5417450; Metro Argüelles). Popular cable car operates Easter to September daily 11am–3pm and 5–10pm; October to March Saturday and Sunday only, noon–3pm and 5–10pm.

Zoo/Aquarium (Casa de Campo; Metro Batán). Open daily, 10.30am–9.30pm (summer), 10.30am–7pm (October to April).

SPORT

Most gyms require membership. Jogging in the parks is pleasant.

A swimming pool is a godsend in summer: **Canal Reina Isabel II** (summer only, Calle Sta Engracia 25, tel: 91 4452000). **Aqualung** (Puerta de la Ermita del Santo 40, tel: 91 4634052) is a heated pool with waves; open Tuesday to Saturday and holidays 10am–10pm. Many *madrileños* go skiing in the sierra in winter. The four main resorts (Navacerrada, Valcotos, Valdesqui and La Pinilla) are around 70km/40 miles from the city.

The main spectator sport is football, for which tickets are usually easily available on the day. Real Madrid's home is Estadio Santiago Bernabeu and Atlético de Madrid's is at Vicente Calderón, Puerta de Virgen del Puerto.

OTHER USEFUL ADDRESSES

Visas (all countries): Calle Los Madrazos 9, tel: 91 5219350.
British Embassy: Calle Fernándo el Santo 16, tel: 91 3080618
Canadian Embassy: Calle Núñez de Balboa 35, tel: 91 4314300
French Embassy: Calle Salustiano Olozaga 9, tel: 91 4312351
German Embassy: Calle Fortuny 8, tel: 91 5579000
US Embassy: Calle Serrano 75, tel: 91 5784586
Tourist information offices: Plaza Mayor 3, tel: 91 3664874; Chamartín railway station, tel: 91 3159976; Barajas airport (international arrivals), tel: 91 3058656

FURTHER READING

The Adventures of Don Quixote, Miguel de Cervantes Saavedra, translated by J.M. Cohen, Penguin, London.
The New Spaniards, John Hooper, Penguin, London.
Spain, Jan Morris, Penguin, London.
Fortunata and Jacinta, Benito Peréz Galdós, Penguin, London.
The Spanish Temper, V S Pritchett, The Hogarth Press, London.
Madrid, A Travellers' Companion, selected and introduced by Hugh Thomas, Constable, London.
Insight Guide: Madrid, Apa Publications, London.

Life on the tiles

Index

A(KПОΠΙ(DGП(ПΙS

Photography	Bill Wassman *and*
Page 8–9	Paca Arceo
76B	Luis Davilla/Cover
Cover	Shaun Egan/Tony Stone Images
Page 79	Wolfgang Fritz
29	Diana Kvaternik/Naturpress
10, 13, 14	José Martin
52	Richard Nowitz
27	Rafa Sanano/Cover
20	Carlos Vegas/Naturpress
36B, 43B, 50, 60B	Jaime Villanueva/Naturpress
Practical Information, Toledo and Crafts itineraries	Juan Datri
Cartography	Berndtson & Berndtson

Insight Guides			
Alaska	Dresden	Marine Life in the	South India
Alsace	Dublin	South China Sea	South Tyrol
Amazon Wildlife	Düsseldorf	Melbourne	Southeast Asia
American Southwest	**E**ast African Wildlife	Mexico	Southeast Asia Wildl
Amsterdam	East Asia	Mexico City	Southern California
Argentina	Eastern Europe	Miami	Southern Spain
Atlanta	Ecuador	Montreal	Spain
Athens	Edinburgh	Morocco	Sri Lanka
Australia	Egypt	Moscow	Sweden
Austria	**F**inland	Munich	Switzerland
Bahamas	Florence	**N**amibia	Sydney
Bali	Florida	Native America	**T**aiwan
Baltic States	France	Nepal	Tenerife
Bangkok	Frankfurt	Netherlands	Texas
Barbados	French Riviera	New England	Thailand
Barcelona	**G**ambia & Senegal	New Orleans	Tokyo
Bay of Naples	Germany	New York City	Trinidad & Tobago
Beijing	Glasgow	New York State	Tunisia
Belgium	Gran Canaria	New Zealand	Turkey
Belize	Great Barrier Reef	Nile	Turkish Coast
Berlin	Great Britain	Normandy	Tuscany
Bermuda	Greece	Northern California	**U**mbria
Boston	Greek Islands	Northern Spain	US National Parks Ea
Brazil	**H**amburg	Norway	US National Parks W
Brittany	Hawaii	**O**man & the UAE	**V**ancouver
Brussels	Hong Kong	Oxford	Venezuela
Budapest	Hungary	Old South	Venice
Buenos Aires	**I**celand	**P**acific Northwest	Vienna
Burgundy	India	Pakistan	Vietnam
Burma (Myanmar)	India's Western	Paris	**W**ales
Cairo	Himalaya	Peru	Washington DC
Calcutta	Indian Wildlife	Philadelphia	Waterways of Europ
California	Indonesia	Philippines	Wild West
Canada	Ireland	Poland	**Y**emen
Caribbean	Israel	Portugal	
Catalonia	Istanbul	Prague	
Channel Islands	Italy	Provence	**Insight Pocket Guide**
Chicago	**J**amaica	Puerto Rico	**A**egean Islands ★
Chile	Japan	**R**ajasthan	Algarve ★
China	Java	Rhine	Alsace
Cologne	Jerusalem	Rio de Janeiro	Amsterdam ★
Continental Europe	Jordan	Rockies	Athens ★
Corsica	**K**athmandu	Rome	Atlanta ★
Costa Rica	Kenya	Russia	**B**ahamas ★
Crete	Korea	**S**t Petersburg	Baja Peninsula ★
Crossing America	**L**isbon	San Francisco	Bali ★
Cuba	Loire Valley	Sardinia	Bali *Bird Walks*
Cyprus	London	Scotland	Bangkok ★
Czech & Slovak	Los Angeles	Seattle	Barbados ★
Republics	**M**adeira	Sicily	Barcelona ★
Delhi, Jaipur, Agra	Madrid	Singapore	Bavaria ★
Denmark	Malaysia	South Africa	Beijing ★
	Mallorca & Ibiza	South America	Berlin ★
	Malta	South Asia	Bermuda ★

nsight Guides

er every major destination in every continent.

Bhutan★
Boston★
British Columbia★
Brittany★
Brussels★
Budapest &
 Surroundings★
Canton★
Chiang Mai★
Chicago★
Corsica★
Costa Blanca★
Costa Brava★
Costa del
Sol/Marbella★
Costa Rica★
Crete★
Denmark★
Fiji★
Florence★
Florida★
Florida Keys★
French Riviera★
Gran Canaria★
Hawaii★
Hong Kong★
Hungary
Ibiza★
Ireland★
Ireland's Southwest★
Israel★
Istanbul★
Jakarta★
Jamaica★
Kathmandu *Bikes &
 Hikes*★
Kenya★
Kuala Lumpur★
Lisbon★
Loire Valley★
London★
Macau
Madrid★
Malacca
Maldives
Mallorca★
Malta★
Mexico City★
Miami★
Milan★
Montreal★
Morocco★
Moscow
Munich★

Nepal★
New Delhi
New Orleans★
New York City★
New Zealand★
Northern California★
Oslo/Bergen★
Paris★
Penang★
Phuket★
Prague★
Provence★
Puerto Rico★
Quebec★
Rhodes★
Rome★
Sabah★
St Petersburg★
San Francisco★
Sardinia
Scotland★
Seville★
Seychelles★
Sicily★
Sikkim
Singapore★
Southeast England
Southern California★
Southern Spain★
Sri Lanka★
Sydney★
Tenerife★
Thailand★
Tibet★
Toronto★
Tunisia★
Turkish Coast★
Tuscany★
Venice★
Vienna★
Vietnam★
Yogyakarta★
Yucatan Peninsula★

**★ = *Insight Pocket
Guides*
with Pull out Maps**

Insight Compact Guides

Algarve
Amsterdam
Bahamas
Bali
Bangkok

Barbados
Barcelona
Beijing
Belgium
Berlin
Brittany
Brussels
Budapest
Burgundy
Copenhagen
Costa Brava
Costa Rica
Crete
Cyprus
Czech Republic
Denmark
Dominican Republic
Dublin
Egypt
Finland
Florence
Gran Canaria
Greece
Holland
Hong Kong
Ireland
Israel
Italian Lakes
Italian Riviera
Jamaica
Jerusalem
Lisbon
Madeira
Mallorca
Malta
Milan
Moscow
Munich
Normandy
Norway
Paris
Poland
Portugal
Prague
Provence
Rhodes
Rome
St Petersburg
Salzburg
Singapore
Switzerland
Sydney
Tenerife
Thailand

Turkey
Turkish Coast
Tuscany
UK regional titles:
 Bath & Surroundings
 Cambridge & East
  Anglia
 Cornwall
 Cotswolds
 Devon & Exmoor
 Edinburgh
 Lake District
 London
 New Forest
 North York Moors
 Northumbria
 Oxford
 Peak District
 Scotland
 Scottish Highlands
 Shakespeare Country
 Snowdonia
 South Downs
 York
 Yorkshire Dales
USA regional titles:
 Boston
 Cape Cod
 Chicago
 Florida
 Florida Keys
 Hawaii: Maui
 Hawaii: Oahu
 Las Vegas
 Los Angeles
 Martha's Vineyard &
  Nantucket
 New York
 San Francisco
 Washington D.C.
Venice
Vienna
West of Ireland

NOTES